Christ Without a Bride?

Michael J. Ray

WestBow
PRESS®
A DIVISION OF THOMAS NELSON
& ZONDERVAN

Copyright © 2019 Michael J. Ray.

All rights reserved. No part of this book may be used or reproduced by any means, graphic, electronic, or mechanical, including photocopying, recording, taping or by any information storage retrieval system without the written permission of the author except in the case of brief quotations embodied in critical articles and reviews.

Unless otherwise indicated, scripture quotations are from the ESV® Bible (The Holy Bible, English Standard Version®), copyright © 2001 by Crossway Bibles, a publishing ministry of Good News Publishers. Used by permission. All rights reserved.

Scripture quotations marked KJV taken from the King James Version of the Bible.

Scripture quotations marked ASV taken from the American Standard Version of the Bible.

WestBow Press books may be ordered through booksellers or by contacting:

WestBow Press
A Division of Thomas Nelson & Zondervan
1663 Liberty Drive
Bloomington, IN 47403
www.westbowpress.com
1 (866) 928-1240

Because of the dynamic nature of the Internet, any web addresses or links contained in this book may have changed since publication and may no longer be valid. The views expressed in this work are solely those of the author and do not necessarily reflect the views of the publisher, and the publisher hereby disclaims any responsibility for them.

Any people depicted in stock imagery provided by Getty Images are models, and such images are being used for illustrative purposes only. Certain stock imagery © Getty Images.

ISBN: 978-1-9736-6259-4 (sc)
ISBN: 978-1-9736-6260-0 (hc)
ISBN: 978-1-9736-6258-7 (e)

Library of Congress Control Number: 2019906627

Printed in the United States of America.

WestBow Press rev. date: 7/18/2019

I have known Mike Ray for over three decades. He is a man who is well qualified to write upon the subject of the New Testament Church. He has served as a minister, deacon, and now as an elder of a local congregation. He comes from a background that gives him unique insight into the meaning of "The Church." He is a zealous laborer in the vineyard of the Lord, giving his time to the building up of the local church numerically and spiritually. You will find his book, Christ Without a Bride a helpful source for your personal devotion, and an excellent workbook for group study. I found his thoughts on "Inside forces that hurt the church," and "outside forces that hurt the church" to be very enlightening, thought provoking, and alarming. Every Evangelist and every elder would do well to read and meditate upon these chapters. The bibliography indicates that a great deal of research, study, and thought have gone into the writing of this book. After reading Christ Without a Bride I think you will agree with the affirmation that he makes, "We cannot go to heaven without the church!

- **Mike Kiser**, Preacher and Elder
Sylacauga Church of Christ
Sylacauga, Alabama

CONTENTS

Author's Preface ix
Dedication xi
Acknowledgments xiii
Introduction..xv

ONE
What Is The Church? 1

TWO
More Descriptions Of The Church 8

THREE
The Church Is Caring..14

FOUR
What The Church Does 21

FIVE
The Church Inspires 30

SIX
What Does Christ Think About The Church?................37

SEVEN
Inside Forces That Hurt The Church............................... 44

EIGHT
Outside Forces That Hurt The Church...........................59

NINE
Religious Division 67

TEN
What Makes A Strong Church? 76

ELEVEN
So How Do We Get A Strong Church? 90

TWELVE
The Church Must Accomplish Its Mission 96

THIRTEEN
The Church, The Gate To Heaven 106

Bibliography 115

AUTHOR'S PREFACE

I love the Lord's church. Many of the best times of my life took place at church. I love the fellowship, seeing the smiles and joy on the faces of people who wish to be good and do good things. Christianity offers one the best life to live. If only we could convince everyone that this life is the best life, what a great world this would be. We would have no wars, no anger, no murders, no robberies, no adultery, no lying, no envy, no bad things, and no sin. Everyone would put others before themselves.

This world is so selfish, so greedy, so hungry for power, but there would be none of those things if we could convince everyone to accept Christ as the master and follow his teachings. He set up the church so that the kingdom on earth would be like the kingdom of heaven. That kingdom, his kingdom, is the church. It is not perfect yet, but it will be when he returns (Rev. 21).

Jesus left a mission for the church to seek and save the lost, just as it was his mission when he left heaven and came to earth (Luke 19:10). He did it so that we could have a better life here and an even greater and eternal life with him in heaven.

It is my hope that this little book will cause someone to know and love Jesus and his church and gain that heavenly home.

DEDICATION

I want to dedicate this book to my Granddad, Homer Erby Ray. He was the greatest religious influence I had during my early years. He spent time with me and set a good example for me even through my time as a heathen. Because of him, I always knew that the things I was doing were wrong.

I also want to dedicate the book to my beautiful wife, Etta. She took over when my Granddad died. She would not go out with me unless I went to church with her. When I joined the Army, Etta wrote to me and sent religious tracts for me to read. She stayed with me when I continued to be a heathen, but her faithfulness finally got the best of me, and I am glad it did. She introduced me to my best friend, Jesus, and he and Etta have supported me for fifty-one years now. What a great life they have given me!

Michael J. Ray

ACKNOWLEDGMENTS

I also want to thank Janie and Michael Giddens for their help in editing this book. They are very busy people, but they took out time for me and for this book. They demonstrated the love and comradery found in the Lord's church. I hope you, the reader, find it too. David and Linda Lipe also were a tremendous help in getting things in order. This book will be much better because of what they did.

All scripture references are from the English Standard Version (ESV) unless otherwise stated.

INTRODUCTION

A few days back, I was looking for an image for a presentation when I saw a sign image that said, "God did not call us to go to church, He called us to be the church." The caption under it read, "God is calling us to be the church." Then, on the same page was the same quote except under it was the caption, "God is calling us *not* to go to church" (Bing Images n. d.). Charles Hodge was right when he said, "People in the world today resent the church and will have nothing to do with it. The tolerant world has no tolerance for the church because the church has no tolerance for their evil ways" (Hodge 2000, 71–72).

> In recent years, the percentage of U.S. adults who say they regularly attend religious services has been declining, while the share of Americans who attend only a few times a year, seldom or never has been growing. A new Pew Research Center survey finds that the main reason people regularly go to church, synagogue, mosque or another house of worship is an obvious one: to feel closer to God. Nevertheless, the things that keep people away from religious services are more complicated.
>
> Among those who attend no more than a few times a year, about three-in-ten say they do not go to religious services for a simple reason: They are not believers. However, a much larger share stays away not because

of a lack of faith, but for other reasons. This includes many people who say one very important reason they do not regularly attend church is that they practice their faith in other ways. Others cite things they dislike about particular congregations or religious services (for example, they have not found a church or house of worship they like, or they do not like the sermons). Still, others name logistical reasons, like being in poor health or not having the time to go, as very important reasons for not regularly attending religious services. (Pew Research Center 2018)

It seems that many in the world, even in the Christian world, are confused about the church. They do not know what the church is, what its purpose is, and what is most important, they do not understand the relationship Jesus has with the church. Hodge goes on to say, "Since 1960 the religious world has proudly said, 'I love Jesus, but I hate the church'" (Hodge 2000, 72). Many today think the church is unnecessary; but what is the church? What is its relationship with Christ, and what role does the church have in God's plan of salvation for all humankind?

Let us do the first things first. You have to go to church to be the church (Acts 2:47, KJV). The Lord adds the saved to the church so the church becomes all the saved people. The Bible also says, "And let us consider one another to provoke unto love and to good works: not neglecting to meet together, as is the habit of some," (Heb. 10:24-25). You cannot provoke one another to love and good works without being with one another. For one to go out and claim to be the church and not go to church is hypocritical. This statement, "God did not call us to go to church, He called us to be the church," could be made truthful by adding just two words, "God did not call us *to just* go to church, He called us to be the church.

The world must learn what the church is, what its relationship to Jesus Christ is, and what its purpose is in God's scheme to save humankind.

ONE

What Is The Church?

It all begins with Matthew 16:15–18, when Jesus says, "Upon this rock," the rock-solid fact that he is the Christ, the Son of God, "I will build my church." It is his church, not some man's church. He said the singular "my church." Paul proclaimed,

> There is one body [i.e., church] and one Spirit–just as you were called to the one hope that belongs to your call–one Lord, one faith, one baptism, one God and Father of all, who is over all and through all and in all. (Eph. 4:4–6)

There is only one body (church), just as there is only one God. The challenge, for everyone, is to find the right one because there are many false teachers in the world. (see Acts 20:28-30; Gal. 1:6-9; 1 Tim. 1:3; 4:1-5; 2 Thess. 2:9-12)

> The true church of Christ is the church Jesus promised to build (Matt. 16:18). It consists of everyone Christ has redeemed. The Lord adds the saved to the church (Acts 2:47 KJV), transfers the redeemed into the kingdom of his beloved Son (Col. 1:13), and makes

each born-again child a part of his family. (Gal. 3:26-27). (C. May, 2012, 59)

The Father appointed Christ to head over his church, "and he put all things under his feet and gave him to be head over all things to the church which is His body, the fullness of Him that fills all in all" (Eph. 1:22). Paul taught the same thing to the church at Colossae when he said,

> Christ is the head of the body, the church: who is the beginning, the firstborn from the dead; that in all things he might have the *preeminence*. For it pleased the Father that in him should all fullness dwell. (Col. 1:18-19)

One cannot help but notice the word *preeminence* in the Colossian passage. The Greek word is *proteuo* (πρωτ□ύω), kin to *protos* (πρῶτος), meaning "First in time or place in any succession of things or persons. First, in rank, influence, and honor" (Smith 1999). Jesus should have the first place in all things, yet many religious organizations do not give him that preeminence-even with the name they call themselves. The names on their meeting places do not give him any honor, and if you ask the members what their religion is, they reply, "I am a ___" Well, they often do not say Christian. They name themselves for a certain procedure they follow or they name themselves after some man. What is wrong with just saying, "I am a Christian"? Christ built his church. He paid for it with his blood (Acts 20:28). Why can't we call ourselves Christians and give our meeting places names that show who owns them, such as Christ's Church, the Christian Church, or the Church of Christ? These would at least give him the preeminence he deserves. Acts 4:12 says, "And there is salvation in no one else, for there is no other name under heaven given among men by which we must be saved."

T. W. Hunt says,

> We who are his subjects must treat Him as the sovereign that He is. He must have the preeminence among His people. "And he is the head of the body, the church. He is the beginning, the firstborn from the dead, that in everything he might be preeminent." (1995, 143–144, including Col. 1:18)

THE CALLED OF GOD

The church is the called out of God. It is the Body of Christ, The Family of God, and the Temple of God. It is an assembly of God's people who work together to further the Kingdom of God in this world. (Lynn 1978, 2).

The church is called by God to be his people. 1 Peter 2:9 says,

> But ye are a chosen generation, a royal priesthood, a holy nation, a peculiar people; that ye should shew forth the praises of him who hath called you out of darkness into his marvelous light. (KJV)

Note the distinctiveness of the word "called."

First, they are a *chosen* people (elected race). They are chosen for salvation. The church is not a building; it is the people in the building. They are the assembly, the *ecclesia*, the ones called out every Sunday for a special day to worship God, and then they do the other things Christians do. They pray, study, help the needy, and proclaim the gospel to the world. God called them by the gospel (2 Thess. 2:14), and the call is issued to all people (Mark 16:15; Matt. 28:19–20; John 3:16). However, God will only choose those who accept the call.

Second, they are a royal priesthood. Under the Law of Moses, the priests were a special class. They all came from the tribe of Levi to officiate in worship. Now, all Christians engage in the worship of God, all are priests, and all can go directly to God for themselves. We do not have to go through another priest to reach God, as another prominent religion requires. Jesus says, "I am the way, the truth, and the life, *no one comes to the Father but by me*" (John 14:6).

Third, they constitute a *holy nation* with Christ as their King. They are holy because they are dedicated to a sacred purpose, *to proclaim* the excellence of God and his salvation.

Paul and Peter both describe the call. Paul states in Romans 1:6, "You are the called of Jesus Christ." And in Colossians 3:15, he tells the Colossian church they were "called in one body… of Christ." Peter also tells his readers that they "were called by His (Christ's) glory and virtue and not their own" (1 Pet. 5:10).

God calls the saints out of darkness into his marvelous light, and they will live a different life. "Darkness" represents a state of sin, but the people of the church who were once in darkness are now in the light of the Lord, and they walk in the light. They walk as children of light (Eph. 5:8). They conform to the likeness of Christ (Rom. 8:29). The church, the assembly, means those who were called of God.

THE BODY OF CHRIST (EPHESIANS 1:22–23)

The body is a symbol of unity. Paul speaks of a people with different gifts, yet they make up the one body (Rom. 12:4–8; cf. 1 Cor. 12:12–29). The church needs every person, every part of the body, to use his or her talents to create love and good deeds. The sharing of the Lord's Supper also illustrates the essential oneness of the members of the church. Several other scriptures identify the church as the body of Christ (see Eph. 1:22–23, 4:12, 15–16; 5:23; Col. 1:18, 23).

God the Father designated Christ as the head of the church, the body, and he must have the preeminence (Col. 1:18). He is the controlling factor and the source of the church's life and fullness. Jesus's death on the cross brought the Jews and Gentiles together into the one body (Eph. 2:16). The fullness of Christ flows through the church, his body, and provides it with life and power (Eph. 1:23; Col. 1:19). As head of the church, Christ exercises Lordship and authority over his body. "He loves the church and gave himself up for it. He sanctifies and washes it so that it becomes glorious and holy. He nourishes the church" (Eph. 5:25–30). And the church subjects itself to him and works with him to present itself as perfect and in full acceptance of the Father's plans to bring all humankind together; people treating one another as members of his body.

THE TEMPLE OF GOD

The Bible also calls the church the Temple of God.

> The presence of God in The Old Testament temple made it holy. The ark was in there, God enthroned Himself there, His name was associated there, and His glory went out from there. From the Temple came revelations to the people, and from the Temple, they received their blessings and salvation. (Minear 1960, 96)

Today, God does not dwell in man-made temples (Acts 17:24). He lives in individual Christians (1 Cor. 6:19) and congregations of his church (1 Cor. 3:16–17) as well as in the whole church worldwide. In Ephesians 2:21, Paul says, "In Christ, all the building fitly framed together grows unto a holy temple in the Lord." One needs just to imagine a place where a group of God-filled Christians meets to worship him and commune with him at the Lord's Supper, singing praise to him and talking to him in prayer. It is a special togetherness, a joyful time, knowing that he is with them because he promises to be (Matt. 18:20). In meetings like this, Christians get genuine encouragement and motivation to continue serving him as they trust him to reward them with the crown of life. Why would you not love this as Christ does?

> Just as God worked in the Old Testament Temple, so He works in the New Testament Temple. From the New Testament Temple (Church) proclamations from his word go out, and from the church, we receive our blessings and our salvation. (Minear 1960, 219)

The church is the most important aspect of God's plan to save humankind. Paul warns the elders of the Ephesian church,

> Take heed unto yourselves, and to all the flock, in which the Holy Spirit hath made you bishops, to feed the church of the Lord which he purchased with his own blood. (Acts 20:28 ASV)

The fact that Jesus paid for the church with his blood renders the church very important. It is his blood that washes away sin, and the only biblical way to encounter the blood is through baptism (Acts 22:16; Rom. 6:1–5; Gal. 3; 27).

CHAPTER ONE QUESTIONS

1. Who built the church?
2. How many churches did he build?
3. Who should have preeminence in the church?
4. How does God call the church (spiritually)?
5. How does Peter describe the church?
6. The body is a symbol of _____.
7. Who is the head of the body?
8. Since God does not dwell in a man-made temple today, where does he dwell?
9. As the temple of God, what does the New Testament Temple do?
10. What did Jesus pay for his church?

TWO

More Descriptions Of The Church

THE CHURCH IS A COMMUNITY OF BELIEVERS

People recognize churches for their faithfulness. Jesus said to his disciples,

> Believe me that I am in the Father, and the Father in me: or else believe me for the very works' sake. Verily, verily, I say unto you, He that believeth on me, the works that I do shall he do also; and greater works than these shall he do; because I go unto my Father. (John 14:11–12, KJV)

The church must fully believe that Jesus is the Christ, the Son of God, that he died on a cross for the sins of humanity, that they buried him, and that God raised him from the dead. Christians believe in God and that "Jesus said, I am the way, the truth, and the life: no man cometh unto the Father, but by me" (John 14:6, KJV). Christians in congregations all over the world have taken the Bible, weighed the evidence and come away with firm confidence in God and the Lordship of Jesus Christ. The Bible says, "Faith comes by hearing the Word of

God" (Romans 10:17). Faith is our common bond with Christ and each other, "The righteous will live by faith" (Gal. 3:11).

We must maintain this faith because without it, we cannot please God (Heb. 11:6, KJV). Again, the Hebrew writer warns us, "For we are made partakers of Christ, if we hold the beginning of our confidence steadfast unto the end; While it is said, Today if ye will hear his voice, harden not your hearts, as in the provocation" (Heb. 3:14–15, KJV). Our faith must also grow because we do not know what trials may lie ahead. Peter warns,

> …who by God's power are being guarded through faith for a salvation ready to be revealed in the last time. In this you rejoice, though now for a little while, if necessary, you have been grieved by various trials. (1Pet. 1:5–6)

Paul's faith is a good example of strong faith. In 2 Corinthians 11:22–28 he reveals the many hardships that he went through to proclaim the gospel to much of the known world. In 12:7–10 he talks about his thorn in the flesh, how he prayed three times for God to remove it, but God told him that his grace was enough for him. Paul had such strong faith that nothing would drive him away from his Lord Jesus Christ, not even this thorn. He expressed his faith as,

> …But I am not ashamed, for I know whom I have believed, and I am convinced that he is able to guard until that Day what has been entrusted to me (2 Tim. 1:12).

Paul's faith, confidence, and assurance were in Christ. He said, "I know 'whom,' not 'what,' I have believed." His faith was in a person, not a system. He said in Romans 7:24, "Wretched man that I am! Who will deliver me from this body of death?" Once again, Paul asks, "Who, not what will deliver me…"

Faith (true, genuine, confident) prompts obedience. "He that believes on the Son has eternal life, but he that obeys not the Son will not see life, but the wrath of God abides on him" (John 3:16, 36, ASV). Is your faith like Paul's faith? Does it consist of a definite experience ("I know")? Is it a personal faith ("I have believed")? Is it a convincing power ("I am persuaded")?

Faith is what moves a person to obedience and when he obeys the gospel, he is added to the church by the Lord (Acts 2:47). The church is a believing community.

THE CHURCH IS COMMITTED

Cyprian to Donatus, 3rd Century AD:

> This seems a cheerful world, Donatus, when I view it from this fair garden under the shadow of these vines. However, if I climbed some great mountain and looked over the wide lands, you know very well what I would see. Brigands on the high road, pirates on the seas, in the amphitheaters men murdered to please the applauding crowds, under all roofs misery and selfishness. It is a nasty world, Donatus, an incredibly bad world. In the midst of it, I have found a quiet and holy people. They have discovered a joy, which is a thousand times better than any pleasures of this sinful life. They are despised and persecuted, but they care not. They have overcome the world. These people, Donatus, are the Christians and I am one of them. (Trish 2009)

The above story takes place in a real, genuine conversation. Can you remember your story, who you were, what happened to you, and who you are now? Jesus knew that there would be a huge price to pay for those who followed him; he knew there would be a need for a comforting community. His teaching was against the ways of the world; "And this is the judgment: the light has come into the world, and people loved the darkness rather than the light because their works were evil" (John 3:19). We can see this in what happened to Cyprian in the third century, and even back in the first century (Acts 7–8), the Jews and Romans were severely persecuting Christians, even those in their own families. Walter Brueggemann says of the first-century church,

> The congregation, as a community in crisis, gathers to decide one more time about its identity and its vocation. The people gathered have been bombarded since the last gathering by other voices of interpretation also wanting to offer identity and a vocation. (1988, 139).

James Thompson offers three reasons for the need of a fellowship: (1) "The first-century congregations would be a community composed of individuals who had left families to become a part of this new family. They could recognize the corporate nature of its faith." (2) "The ancient communities shared a common story that involved pain and suffering, which resulted in a corporate consciousness that we all long to share." (3) "To preach is to act ecclesiastically, to build on the supposition that the body of listeners intends to believe and take action as a community" (2001, 96–97).

Christians in a congregation belong to one another and to Christ, but they do not know and feel what this means. They need to discover the meaning of commitment to the body of Christ.

The prophet Jeremiah says,

> Then I said, I will not make mention of him, nor speak any more in his name. But his word was in mine heart as a burning fire shut up in my bones, and I was weary with forbearing, and I could not stay. (20:9, KJV)

The church needs more Jeremiahs who have a fire in their heart for God and his church. Will you be a Jeremiah and help the church grow? Paul tells us how to act in the community of believers:

> Love one another with brotherly affection. Outdo one another in showing honor. Do not be slothful in zeal; be fervent in spirit, serve the Lord. Rejoice in hope, be patient in tribulation, be constant in prayer. Contribute to the needs of the saints and seek to show hospitality. (Rom. 12:10–13)

The church needs more people who fit Paul's standards. Leonard Ravenhill calls Paul an empire builder for God, and he tells of the event when Paul met the Lord on the road to Damascus: "Paul, this fire eating religious zealot met the fire baptizing Lord; and as a result, when Saul was changed, civilization took a turn for the better" (1959, 115). Jesus knew it would be difficult to follow him, so he set up a system to help us remain faithful and spread the word of his love and sacrifice. This system is the congregations of the Christian church. Be like Jeremiah and Paul, standing up for God's ways. People in the world need to understand this so they can love the church as they do Jesus.

Jesus provided two parables that illustrate the wisdom of knowing the price of following him. First, see the cost before you start building to be sure you have enough money to finish, or else the people will mock you. Second, before you go to war, be sure you have enough strength to win; if you do not, you will have the humiliation of defeat (Luke 14:28–32). Jesus wants us to understand the costs before we join him because there could be some suffering involved, and the consequences of leaving him are catastrophic. The Bible compares the one who deserts Jesus to pigs returning to their mire and a dog to his vomit (2 Pet. 2:22).

Jesus proclaims that whoever is not willing to bear his cross and come after him cannot be his disciple. Will you take up the cross and follow Jesus?

CHAPTER TWO QUESTIONS

1. People recognize churches by their _____.
2. How do we find faith? (Rom. 10:17)
3. How do the righteous live?
4. What does it mean to live by faith?
5. How long must we maintain our faith? (Heb. 11:6; 3:14–15)
6. Describe Paul's faith. (2 Tim. 1:12)
7. Explain Jeremiah 20:9.
8. Describe holiness in your own words.
9. How do we demonstrate holiness today? (2 Pet. 1:5–11)
10. Why should we be compassionate? (Phil. 2:5; Mark 12:25–31; Matt. 14:14; 13:32)

THREE

The Church Is Caring

THE CHURCH IS COMPASSIONATE

As such a community, the church aids people with various problems by serving their physical and spiritual needs. Compassion involves sympathy for others and deep concern for them. It is based on the second greatest commandment: "Love your neighbor as yourself" (Mark 12:28–31). It involves unselfish concern for the good of others.

Jesus was compassionate. In Matthew 14:14, "He saw a great crowd and had compassion on them and healed their sick." In Matthew 15:32, Jesus said, "I have compassion on the crowd because they have been with me three days and have nothing to eat. And I am unwilling to send them away hungry, lest they faint on the way." Luke also tells us in 7:13, when the widow Nain's son dies and she is weeping, the Lord saw her and "He had compassion on her and said to her, 'Do not weep.'" Matthew 9 is the chapter on compassion, in which Jesus heals a paralytic by saying, "Take heart, my son; your sins are forgiven." Of course, this miracle also proves that he had the power to forgive sin. However, it did get him in trouble with Jewish leaders who happened to be there, but with his compassion, he healed the man, knowing that it would put him in jeopardy with the Jewish officials. In verses 10–13, Jesus takes another risk by eating with publicans and sinners and when challenged by the Pharisees, he explained, "Those who are well have no need of a physician, but those who are sick." Verses 18–26 tell the tender story of Jairus' daughter and the woman with an issue of blood. In verses 27–31, Jesus gives sight to two blind men. In verses 32–34, he heals a dumb man possessed by demons. In the final paragraph of verses 35–38, Jesus: continues to preach the gospel of the kingdom and healing diseases (35); has compassion for the people and says, "They are like sheep led to the slaughter" (36); points out that the harvest is plentiful, but the laborers are few (37), meaning there were many people who needed teaching, but only a few workers to take care of them. Finally, he tells his disciples to pray that the Lord sends workers (38). Jesus was very compassionate; he wanted to help anyone who needed it. If Jesus had compassion, should not his followers have the same mind? Remember, in Philippians 2:5, Paul says, "Have this mind among yourselves, which is yours in Christ." Compassion drove Jesus to action. The church today should be motivated by Christ to have compassion for others. But compassion is more than simply feeling sorry for someone; it is taking action to relieve them of their injury, whether it is physical or spiritual. Jesus acted in three ways to make his church compassionate. He taught them and demonstrated to them how to practice compassion. He preached to them concerning the kingdom and evangelism and carrying the message of salvation to people. He healed the sick and fed the hungry. He taught by example.

Churches try to do the same thing today. They cannot perform miracles to heal people, but they can provide food and medicine, counsel, and service. They can and do offer help for sickness, hunger, clothing, and many other things, both physical and spiritual.

I had the privilege to go to Panama with medical mission teams for seven years. I received support from four great congregations of the Lord's church who had compassion for the needy. On these trips, we had an ophthalmologist who performed cataract surgeries for over a hundred people. Many of those people were completely blind. One day, after he had operated on an older blind man, the doctor took the bandages off and held up two fingers, and asked the man how many fingers he could see. The man said, "dos" (two). The doctor held up four fingers and asked him how many fingers could he see. He said, "quatro" (four) and then began dancing all around the room. The audiologist would check the Panamanian ears. Most of them needed clean outs, but four of them had physical problems with their ears. They needed hearing aids, and the audiologist had brought some with him. He set up the hearing aids and gave them to all four Panamanians, and they could hear.

Then there is the story about Elena Pimentel. Manuel and Elena took good care of my partner, Larry Brady, and myself. We had been staying with them for two weeks when Elena went to the doctor in Panama City. Larry had also gone to Panama City that day, so I was alone with the Pimentel family when Elena got home. Manuel and Elena were trying to understand what the diagnosis was based on the doctor's report, but they could not figure it out, so I asked them to let me see it. What I saw was a big word I could understand – leprosy. I called another missionary who was staying north of us and told him about it, and he said, "Mike, you guys will have to get out of there." I called Larry in Panama City, and he said the same thing. The entire Pimentel family was afraid and crying, as was I. We cried and cried and cried. I called Larry back again and told him that we could not leave them, that we had already been staying with them for two weeks and if we were going to get it, we had already been exposed. He agreed, and we continued to stay with them. Larry called our medical administrator back in the States and the CDC. They told us it was okay to stay because leprosy was very hard to catch. We were not too worried about it after that, but Elena had to take strong medication for almost a year before she was clear. Larry helped her get the medicine. He heads a great organization called the Panama Mission and is very good at helping the Panamanians lead a better life.

The other medical professionals had patients with cuts, bruises, colds, broken bones, and other ailments, and they did a good job of taking care of them. But that wasn't all we did. We also repaired and built houses, poured concrete floors in homes that had mud floors, and above all, we taught the gospel to the people, many of whom obeyed it. I tried to go out with the Panamanian preachers every chance I had to do some teaching myself, and there is no better feeling than to teach someone and have them obey the gospel.

I enjoyed all the trips to Panama, but this particular one was special because I could say that we helped the blind regain their sight, the lame to walk, the lepers to be cleansed, the deaf to hear, and the poor to have the good news preached to them. We did everything that Jesus told John the Baptist's disciples to tell John in Matthew 11:4–5:

> And Jesus answered them, "Go and tell John what you hear and see; the blind receive their sight and the lame walk, lepers are cleansed, and the deaf hear, and the dead are raised, and the poor have the good news preached to them."

Well, we did not raise any dead people, but we did do all the other things Jesus did; not in the same way he did, of course, but it was great!

We would have around thirty to thirty-five people with us on these trips, and every one of them got support from one, two, or even more churches who had compassion for the needs of people all over the world. These churches have the mind of Christ and want to serve humankind and teach them about God's love

THE CHURCH IS A HOLY COMMUNITY

Holiness is next to Godliness. "The ordinary Hebrew word for holy is *Kadosh,* separated. It is represented in the New Testament by the Greek word *Agios*. It is used for what is set apart from common to sacred use" (Davis 1980, 334). The utensils used in the Old Testament Temple had to be washed to be made holy and set apart for use in God's house. Today, baptism does the same thing for Christians. We have to be cleansed, have our sins washed away (Acts 22:16), to be used in God's kingdom.

"The church makes God's image known to the world today" (Lynn 1978, 2). The Bible says, "In Christ Jesus, the whole structure is joined together and grows into a holy temple in the Lord" (Eph. 2:20–21).

Christians must maintain a lifestyle such that the world can see God through them. Godliness is somewhat like God-like-ness; not that Christians have a great power that God has, but they must have the character that he does and they must demonstrate that character to the world. Jesus tells us "let your light shine before men, that they may see your good works, and glorify your Father who is in Heaven" (Matt. 5:16).

Jesus made the Father known with his life (John 14:7–15), and he instructed his disciples to do the same. Jesus also pointed out to his disciples that they must love him and obey his commands (v. 15). The new life is living like Christ, showing the world God by obedience to him.

Every person who obeys the gospel should lead a changed life. Paul teaches us what this process is.

First, we cannot continue to live a life filled with sin, thinking that grace will redeem it all. That cannot happen because we were supposed to die for sin and should not continue to live in it. Since those baptized into Christ are baptized into his death, they bury the old person (spiritually) and are resurrected like Christ to walk in a new life. In this way, we unite with Christ in his death and if so will be with him in a resurrection like his (Rom. 6:1–5). Paul continued to teach this message everywhere he went. His teaching of Titus was another example, when he revealed that "Jesus has saved us, not because of righteous things we have done, but because of his mercy. He saved us through the washing of rebirth and renewal of the Holy Spirit" (Titus 3:5).

Second, Peter also tells us how to be holy:

> For this very reason, make every effort to supplement your faith with virtue, and virtue with knowledge, and knowledge with self-control, and self-control with steadfastness, and steadfastness with godliness, and godliness with brotherly affection, and brotherly affection with love. For if these qualities are yours and are increasing, they keep you from being ineffective or

unfruitful in the knowledge of our Lord Jesus Christ. For whoever lacks these qualities is so nearsighted that he is blind, having forgotten that he was cleansed from his former sins. Therefore, brothers, be all the more diligent to confirm your calling and election, for if you practice these qualities, you will never fall. For in this way there will be richly provided for you an entrance into the eternal kingdom of our Lord and Savior Jesus Christ. (2 Pet. 1:5–11)

"Unholy people do not think holy thoughts" (Hunt 1995, 17). The first step towards having the mind of Christ is to train oneself to concentrate on the holy. Christians must concentrate on Christ and the holiness he demands. When we wander from those thoughts, sin is at the door and moves right in. Paul refers to this when he says,

> For those who live according to the flesh set their minds on the things of the flesh, but those who live according to the Spirit set their minds on the things of the Spirit. For to set the mind on the flesh is death but to set the mind on the Spirit is life and peace. (Rom. 8:5–6).

CHAPTER THREE QUESTIONS

1. What does compassion involve?
2. List three passages where Jesus was compassionate.
3. Matthew 9 is appropriately labeled as the _____.
4. What power was revealed by the healing of the paralytic?
5. Why did Jesus eat with the tax collectors and sinners?
6. What does Jesus mean when he said, "the harvest is plentiful, but the laborers are few"?
7. Compassion _____ Jesus to action, and since we have the mind of Christ, it should _____ us (the church) to action.
8. Compassion is more than feeling sorry for a person; it means _____.
9. What three ways did Jesus use to make his church compassionate?
10. List things you can do to demonstrate your compassion.
11. Holy is something that sets apart from a common to a _____ use.
12. The Bible says, "In Christ Jesus, the whole structure is joined together and grows into a _____ temple." Remember the temple today is the church.
13. Jesus made the Father known with his life. What traits do you have that reveal God to the world?
14. List and memorize the nine traits that Peter says will make you holy. (2 Pet. 1:5–8)
15. Why can't people with unholy minds understand holy thoughts?

FOUR

What The Church Does

THE CHURCH WORSHIPS GOD

"To worship is to make obeisance, do reverence. It is used as an act of homage or reverence" (Vine n.d.). The object in the worship of the church must be the one true and living God. "For thou shalt worship no other god: for the LORD, whose name is Jealous, is a jealous God" (Exod. 34:14, KJV). "Oh come, let us worship and bow down; let us kneel before the LORD, our Maker! For he is our God, and we are the people of his pasture, and the sheep of his hand. Today, if you hear his voice, do not harden your hearts…" (Ps. 95:6–8a).

The Christian Church must worship that same God. The apostle Paul explains to the Athenians,

> Now what you worship as something unknown, I am going to proclaim to you. The God who made the world and everything in it, being Lord of heaven and earth, does not live in temples made by man. (Acts 17:23–24)

He also told the Philippian church, "For we are the circumcision, who worship by the Spirit of God and glory in Christ Jesus and put no confidence in the flesh" (Phil. 3:3). The church worships the one true and living God because he is our Maker and God. "Fear God and give him glory, because the hour of judgment has come. Worship him who made the heavens, the earth, the sea, and the springs of water" (Rev. 14:7). We worship him because he loves us (John 3:16), provides salvation for us (Rom. 5:8), shows his love for us in that while we were still sinners, he died for us. Only Christ can do that for us.

> Neither is there salvation in any other: for there is none other name under heaven given among men whereby we must be saved. (Acts 4:12, KJV)

The Christian system of worship is different from the Israeli system. Israel worships according to the Law of Moses. The Christian system worships through Christ, and there is a significant difference. "God made us alive together with him, having forgiven us all our trespasses, by canceling the record of debt that stood against us with its legal demands. This he set aside, nailing it to the cross" (Col. 2:13b–14). Therefore, under the Christian system, it is the Words of Christ that judge us (John 12:48). Jesus also said, "I am the way, and the truth, and the life. No one comes to the Father except through me" (John 14:6). He also told the woman at the well how worship would change under the Christian system. "Our fathers worshiped on this mountain, but you say that in Jerusalem is the place where people ought to worship" (John 4:20). Jesus answered:

> Woman, believe me, the hour is coming when neither on this mountain nor in Jerusalem will you worship the Father. You worship what you do not know; we worship what we know, for salvation is from the Jews. But the hour is coming and is here now when the true worshipers will worship the Father in spirit and truth, for the Father is seeking such people to worship him. God is a spirit, and those who worship him must worship in spirit and truth. (John 4:21-24)

The Hebrew writer speaks of how much better the worship system is under Christ: "But now hath he obtained a more excellent ministry, by how much also he is the mediator of a better covenant, which was established upon better promises" (Heb. 8:6, KJV).

Homage is another aspect of worship. It deals with faith and attitude (the innermost part of the heart). Jesus says,

> These people honor me with their lips, but their heart is far from me; in vain do they worship me, teaching as doctrines the commandments of men. (Matt.15:8–9)

Peter describes it beautifully:

> You also, like living stones, are being built into a spiritual house to be a holy priesthood offering spiritual sacrifices acceptable to God through Jesus Christ. (1 Pet. 2:5)

The heart is important in worship, and we are not referring to the organ in the chest; we are talking about the inner person, the heart of hearts. Worship must come from the heart, or it is not worship at all. Four good things should happen in every worship service:

Joy (Rom. 14:17, KJV): "For the kingdom of God is not meat and drink; but righteousness, and peace, and joy in the Holy Ghost."

Humbleness (1 Pet. 5:6): "Humble yourselves, therefore, under the mighty hand of God so that at the proper time he may exalt you."

Serious (1 Cor. 6:20): "For you were bought with a price. So glorify God in your body."

Helpful: "Obedience makes one feel good; Opportunity to learn and grow; Fellowship with God and Christians is reassuring." (Lynn 1978, 3)

God demands worship, (Matt. 4:10). Jesus said to him, "Be gone, Satan! For it is written, 'You shall worship the Lord your God, and he only shall you serve.'"

God deserves our worship, obedience, and homage. God must be present in the right place in our lives. When he is, we will worship him with good motives, and that will produce a great reward–worshipping in heaven.

Isaiah lifted God high (Isa. 6:1–8). God deserves to be high and lifted in all our eyes. Revelations. 4:8–11 gives an example of how God is worshipped in Heaven:

> And the four living creatures, each of them with six wings, and full of eyes all around and within; and day and night they never cease to say, "holy. Holy, holy, is the Lord God Almighty, who was and is and is to come!" And whenever the living creatures give glory and honor and thanks to him who is seated on the throne, who lives forever and ever, the twenty-four elders fall down before him who is seated on the throne and worship him who lives forever and ever. They cast their crowns before the throne, saying, "Worthy are you, our Lord and God, to receive glory and honor and power, for you created all things, and by your will, they existed and were created."

Jesus, himself said, "The greatest commandment is to love the Lord with all your heart, with all your soul and with all your mind" (Matt. 22:37).

Worship should be done with a pure motive also. If we have God high and lifted up, our motives will be pure, and we will worship him because we love him. John proclaims we love him (God), because he first loved us, (1 John. 4:19). "God shows his love for us in that while we were still sinners, Christ died for us" (Rom. 5:8), and that is not all of it.

> Oh come, let us sing to the Lord; let us make a joyful noise to the rock of our salvation! Let us come into his presence with thanksgiving; let us make a joyful noise to him with songs of praise! For the Lord is a

great God and a great King above all gods. In his hand are the depths of the earth; the heights of the mountains are his also. The sea is his, for he made it, and his hands formed the dry land. Oh come, let us worship and bow down; let us kneel before the Lord, our Maker! For he is our God, and we are the people of his pasture, and the sheep of his hand. Today, if you hear his voice, do not harden your heart. (Ps. 95:1–8a)

There is no greater hope than the hope of a home in heaven. When my daughter was around ten, she was riding in the car with me, and I said, "I wish something would happen." I do not remember now what I wished for, but I remember what she said. "Oh daddy, don't wish for it; hope for it." To which I replied, "Well, what is the difference?" She said, "If you wish, it might not come true, but if you hope for it, it will come true." Well, I was skeptical about the coming true part, but, "hope" in the Bible has a certainty to it. It has that certainty because it has God standing behind the promise that created the hope. One might not have seen the fulfillment of the hope of heaven yet, but one can be certain that God will fulfill it. God grants great and wonderful rewards to those who believe, trust, and obey him.

> Then I looked, and behold, on Mount Zion stood the Lamb, and with him 144,000 who had his name and his Father's name written on their foreheads, and I heard a voice from heaven like the roar of many waters and like the sound of thunder. The voice I heard was like the sound of harpists playing on their harps, and they were singing a new song before the throne, and before the four living creatures and before the elders. No one could learn that song except the 144,000 who had been redeemed from the earth. It is these who have not defiled themselves with women, for they are virgins. It is these who follow the Lamb wherever he goes. These have been redeemed from humankind as

first fruits for God and the Lamb, and in their mouth, no lie was found, for they are blameless. Then I saw another angel flying directly overhead, with an eternal gospel to proclaim to those who dwell on the earth, to every nation and tribe and language and people. And he said with a loud voice, "Fear God and give him glory, because the hour of his judgment has come, and worship him who made heaven and earth, the sea and the springs of water." (Rev. 14:1–7)

The church worships the one true and living God.

The Church Proclaims the Gospel

"The church is a divine creation set for the announcing of the acts of God. Its proclamation is on behalf of the redemption of humankind and the glory of God" (Lynn 1978). Ephesians 3:8–11 tells us that God planned all this, "so that through the church the manifold wisdom of God might now be made known to the rulers and authorities in the heavenly places."

The redemption of humankind is the reason Jesus came to this earth. Jesus said himself that he came to "seek and to save the lost" (Luke 19:10). The apostle Paul proclaimed this message to the church in Rome letting them know that they were, "Being justified freely by his grace through the redemption that is in Jesus Christ" (Rom. 3:24). Paul also proclaimed this to the church in Colossae encouraging them with the words, "In Christ, we have our redemption through his blood, even the forgiveness of sin" (Col. 1:14). Paul said to Titus, "Jesus gave himself for us, that he might redeem us from all iniquity" (Titus 2:14). He proclaimed to the church in Ephesus, "In Christ, we have our redemption through his blood" (Eph. 1:7). The Hebrew writer also proclaimed to his audience that "Christ entered once for all into the holy places, not by means of the blood of goats and calves but by means of his own blood, thus securing an eternal redemption" (Heb. 9:12). Jesus came into this world proclaiming salvation for humankind through his blood, and the apostles continued to proclaim that the salvation of humankind occurred through the blood of Christ. Now, the church must continue the proclamation that salvation is through the blood of Jesus Christ. Paul tells the church that we are a "chosen people for God's possession, zealous for good works" (Titus 2:14b). Jesus commanded his disciples to "Go therefore, and make disciples of all nations, baptizing them in the name of the Father and of the Son and the Holy Spirit, teaching them to observe all that I have commanded you. And behold, I am with you always, to the end of the age" (Matt. 28:19–20). The same was the case with passing the keys to the kingdom (Matt. 16:18–19). Now, the proclamation tasks are passed down to the church for the redemption of mankind.

However, it is not just for the redemption of humankind; it is also for the glory of God. Telling the story of Jesus involves the history of mankind and how God deals with people, with miracles and the development of the plan of salvation. By doing this, God is glorified and people see his majesty. The congregation must have a sound understanding that it is called to proclaim the acts of God. The church also must have the same desire as the apostles. Luke shows the dedication of the apostles when threatened by Jewish leadership to stop proclaiming Christ. Peter and John bravely responded, "Whether it is right in the sight of God to listen to you rather than to God, you must judge, for we cannot but speak of what we have seen and heard" (Acts 4:19–20). "The persecution in Jerusalem was so terrible that they were scattered abroad…" (Acts 8:4). Also, the apostle Paul suffered many trials, but he still proclaimed, "For though I preach the gospel, I have nothing to glory of: for necessity is laid upon me; yea, woe is unto me, if I preach not the gospel!" (1 Cor. 9:16, KJV). The church must see the necessity to encourage each other and seek opportunities (Luke 15:7, 10, 32; Matt. 21:17–26, 32). The church must be willing to do this even in the face of persecution.

The church also must have an accurate conception of the content of proclamation. It is necessary for the teaching of gospel facts to be true because it affects the redemption of humankind and because there are many false teachers in the world (Gal. 1:6–9). Paul warns the church at Thessalonica,

> Let no one deceive you in any way. For that day will not come, unless the rebellion comes first, and the man of lawlessness is revealed, the son of destruction, who opposes and exalts himself against every so-called god or object of worship, so that he takes his seat in the temple of God, proclaiming himself to be God. (2 Thess. 2:3–4)

He also warned Timothy of the false teachers (1 Tim. 4:1–3). Because of these false teachers and the bad situations some people get in, the church faces great danger. It must be ready to answer anyone who asks about its teachings, but "The church has a dual responsibility about the world around us. On the one hand, we are to live, serve, and evangelize in the world. On the other, we are to avoid becoming contaminated by the world" (Stott 2001, 17). The Corinthian church was reminded of this also.

> Now I would remind you, brothers, of the gospel I preached, which you received, and in which you stand, and by which you are saved if you hold fast to the word I preached to you as of first importance what I also received. That Christ died for our sins in accordance with the scriptures, that he was buried, that he was raised on the third day in accordance with the scripture. (1 Cor. 15:1–4)

The church must express its total affirmation to this gospel message to build up the whole and teach it to the world.

CHAPTER FOUR QUESTIONS

1. Define worship.
2. List two reasons to worship God.
3. Where is the scripture reference for, "No one comes to the Father but by me"?
4. What did Jesus tell the Samaritan woman about the new way to worship in the new covenant?
5. Jesus came into the world proclaiming mankind is saved through his _____.
6. Who took over the job after he returned to heaven?
7. Who took it over after they died?
8. Who gets the glory when a soul is saved?
9. List the scripture where the apostles risked their lives to carry out the mission to teach salvation through the blood of Christ.
10. Give reasons why our proclamation must be accurate.

FIVE

The Church Inspires

> As an encouraging or inspiring community, the church functions to lift the human spirit. Its tasks then are to contribute to the building of human spirits in the Christian graces and to see that efforts are made to spread enthusiasm for Christian living and service. (Lynn 1978, 2)

> But exhort one another every day, as long as it is called today, that the deceitfulness of sin may harden none of you. (Heb. 3:13)

> And let us consider how to stir up one another to love and good works, not neglecting to meet together, as is the habit of some, but encouraging one another, and all the more as you see the Day drawing near. (Heb. 10:24–25)

The church must teach and do things that encourages its members. To inspire is to provoke, to move someone to feel good and to do good. Too many people go home from church and all they do is point out the negative. They say things like the singing was flat, the announcements were mixed up, the sermon was boring, the offering was off, it was too hot, and the sound person had the sound too low. Where is our mind? It should be on 2 Peter 1:3-11:

> His divine power has granted to us all things that pertain to life and godliness, through the knowledge of him who called us to his glory and excellence. By which he has granted to us his precious and very great promises, so that through them you may become partakers of the divine nature, having escaped from the corruption that is in the world because of sinful desire. For this very reason, make every effort to supplement your faith with virtue, knowledge, self-control, steadfastness, godliness, brotherly affection, and love. For if these qualities are yours and are increasing, they keep you from being ineffective or unfruitful in the knowledge of our Lord Jesus Christ. For whoever lacks these qualities is so nearsighted that he is blind, having forgotten that he was cleansed from his former sins. Therefore, brothers, be all the more diligent to confirm your calling and election, for if you practice these qualities, you will never fall. For in this way there will be richly provided for you an entrance into the eternal kingdom of our Lord and Savior Jesus Christ.

Why are all the promises in these verses not enough to inspire? God has done his part—it is the best part. Mankind's work is merely contributory but essential, since God's part is done on the condition that mankind complies. Peter instructs us to be diligent, to hasten, to bring in our work. We never know what time may bring us, so we need to act quickly to build ourselves and be ready for our entrance into the eternal kingdom of our Lord.

We can build ourselves in three ways: (1) by encouraging one another by giving each other courage, hope, and confidence, we strengthen, support, and help each other. (2) By inspiring each other. To inspire is, "To infuse into; to affect, as with a superior or supernatural influence; to fill with what animates, enlivens, or exalts; to communicate inspiration to" (Dryden 2014). (3) We build each other up with the promotion of spiritual growth. Peter wrote to inspire his readers to grow in the aspects he mentioned. He was building them up, encouraging them, and inspiring them to practice these things. Paul says, "So then let us pursue what makes for peace and mutual upbuilding" (Rom. 14:9). He also taught the Corinthian church to "do only those things that edify. Let no one seek their own, but let each his neighbor's good" (1 Cor. 10:23–24). He also told them that, "knowledge puffs up, but love edifies" (1 Cor. 8:1). Heaven is a great place and knowing it is there inspires and encourages (1 Thess. 4:13–5:11).

Hearts Set Free – 1 Corinthians 15:8–10

The apostle Paul inspires me. F. F. Bruce wrote a biography of Paul, titled *Paul, Apostle of the Heart Set Free* (Bruce 1977, n.p.) He was free of the Law, free of sin, and had won freedom over death. Yet he called himself a bonded servant of Christ and a slave (Rom. 1; Phil 1; Titus 1). How was that? Paul did it by being so committed to Christ; he was so grateful for what Christ did for him that he had to show his love for him. It was the love of Christ that enslaved Paul. John wrote in 1 John 4:19, "We love because he first loved us." That was certainly true for the apostle Paul. He knew his freedom and salvation came from Christ, and it motivated him.

> In little more than ten years, Paul established the Church in four provinces of the Empire, Galatia, Macedonia, Achaia, and Asia. Before A.D. 47 there were no Churches in these provinces; in A.D; 57 Paul could speak as if his work was done, and could plan extensive tours into the far West without anxiety lest the Churches which he had founded might perish

in his absence for want of his guidance and support. (Bruce 1977, 18)

Let's take a look at Paul's background. He was born Saul of Tarsus in the city of Tarsus. God would change his name to Paul later. He was:

> circumcised on the eighth day, of the people of Israel, of the tribe of Benjamin, a Hebrew of Hebrews; as to the law, a Pharisee; as to zeal, a persecutor of the church; as to righteousness under the law, blameless. But whatever gain I had, I counted as loss for the sake of Christ. (Phil. 3:5–7)

People search all around them for help to solve all kinds of problems. They try everything, even drugs, to help them through hard times. But we have been through this before; only Jesus can help us get over these things. Only Jesus can cleanse humankind and thereby the world. Jesus did that for Paul.

Paul would never forget his past, but it did not bother him since Christ washed it away with his blood. Neither did he like to boast about all that he had done and the hardships he went through to do them unless he had to defend himself (2 Cor. 11; 16b–17; 21b, 30; 12:7–10). He had two reasons for this: (1) He was born "out of due season," meaning that he was the last apostle chosen and (2) because he was the worst of the persecutors against the church. In Romans 7:7–25, Paul describes the difficulty of being righteous under the Law of Moses and he ends his description with this statement "Wretched man that I am! Who will deliver me from this body of death? Thanks be to God through Jesus Christ our Lord!" (Rom. 7:24–25a). The question is a rhetorical one. Paul knew who saved him. He realized that he would have been lost if Jesus had not come, and he was extremely grateful that he did and acknowledged it.

> But by the grace of God I am what I am: and his grace which was bestowed upon me was not in vain;

but I laboured more abundantly than they all: yet not I, but the grace of God which was with me. (1 Cor.15:10, KJV)

Paul knew that the Lord did not have to pick him. God could have let him go on, but the Lord chose him for this very difficult and important work.

For you have heard of my former life in Judaism, how I persecuted the church of God violently and tried to destroy it. And I was advancing in Judaism beyond many of my own age among my people, so extremely zealous was I for the traditions of my fathers. But when he who had set me apart before I was born, and who called me by his grace, was pleased to reveal his Son to me, in order that I might preach him among the Gentiles, I did not immediately consult with anyone. (Gal. 1:13–16)

God's grace was not in vain for the apostle Paul. He acknowledged it. "I worked harder than any of them, though it was not I, but the grace of God that is with me" (1 Cor.15:10c). He led an exemplary life. "What you have learned and received and heard and seen in me—practice these things, and the God of peace will be with you" (Phil. 4:9). He was exceptional. He wrote fourteen epistles, founded many, many churches, and suffered greatly in trying to bring the Kingdom of God into this world. He was completely in the service of Christ. In Philippians 3:7–8, Paul says, "But whatever gain I had, I counted as loss for the sake of Christ. Indeed, I count everything as loss because of the surpassing worth of knowing Christ Jesus my Lord. For his sake, I have suffered the loss of all things and count them as rubbish, in order that I may gain Christ."

Paul did not write about the life of Christ; he demonstrated it with his life, the cost of which was prison and death. He thought it better to be a prisoner of the Lord for a few years than to be the devil's prisoner in hell for all eternity. He committed himself to a complete, costly consecration to Christ. In Galatians 6:17, he said, "From now on let no one cause me trouble, for I bear on my body the marks of Jesus."

Leonard Ravenhill said about Paul,

Paul was sold out to God. Every beat of his heart, every thought in his mind, every step of his feet, and every longing of his soul – all were for Christ and the salvation of humankind. He upset synagogues, had revivals and riots – either one or the other, sometimes both. We seem to have neither. (1959, 119)

Paul said to Agrippa, "Whether short or long, I would to God that not only you but also all who hear me this day might become such as I am, except for these chains" (Acts 26:29). Our wish for all people should be the same as Paul's. If it were so, the church would be much better off today.

CHAPTER FIVE QUESTIONS

1. Who/what inspires you? Whom do you inspire?
2. Define "inspire."
3. Does Hebrews 3:13; 10:24–25; and 2 Peter 1:3–11 inspire you?
4. Do you do what Paul says to do in Romans 14:9; 1 Corinthians 10:23–24; 8:1?
5. List three ways we build one another up. Do these promises inspire you?
6. Which apostle was the wretched man, and why did he feel that way?
7. Are you inspired by all that the apostle Paul accomplished? Please write yes or no.
8. Paul thought it would be better to be a _____ of Christ than to be a prisoner in hell for all eternity.
9. Can you obey the command to move people to love and do good work when you are not present at the meetings? (Heb. 13:3; 10:24–23)

SIX

What Does Christ Think About The Church?

CHRIST'S ATTITUDE TOWARD THE CHURCH

We can see the importance of the church by examining Christ's attitude towards it. Christians are supposed to have the mind of Christ. They are supposed to grow to think as Jesus thought. The apostle Paul puts it as, "Have this mind in you which also was in Christ Jesus who gave up Heaven to set in motion this plan to save humankind" (Phil. 2:5 my paraphrase). Paul also told the church at Corinth, "...that we have the mind of Christ." The mind of Christ thinks like Christ. George Barna writes, "A biblical worldview is thinking like Jesus. It is a way of making our faith practical to every situation we face each day. A biblical worldview is a way of dealing with the world such that we act like Jesus twenty-four hours a day because we think like Jesus" (Barna 2003, 4). So, if Christ intimately aligns himself with the church (Eph. 5:22–23), so should we. If Christ loves the church, so should we, if he cherishes and nourishes the church, so should we. Christians should be happy to be a member of the Lord's church, and they should work to help it grow both physically and spiritually.

Jesus sees the members of the church, the body, as himself (Eph. 1:22–23; Col. 1:24). Therefore, things that affect the body affect Christ. In Acts 9:1–5, Saul (later to become the apostle Paul) persecutes

Christians, yet Christ says he is hurting him. The hurt Saul was inflicting on Christians was also felt by Christ. Jesus even told some of his followers that when they did something, good or bad, to any of his brothers, they did it to him (Matt. 25:40f). In Luke 10:16, Jesus says, "He that hears you hears me, and he who rejects you rejects me." That is, when we hurt the church, the body, the people of Christ, we also hurt Christ. Therefore, when we do not attend church services, it hurts the church and Jesus. When we do not live right by doing things that make the church and the cause of Christ look bad, we also hurt Christ. When we have hatred and resentment in our heart, Jesus feels it too. Anything we do in the church (body) is done to Jesus also, whether it is good or bad.

What those who say that they love Jesus but do not love the church are really saying is that they do not love the brethren. Please note what Jesus says about that:

> If anyone says, "I love God," and hates his brother, he is a liar for he who does not love his brother whom he has seen cannot love God whom he has not seen. Moreover, this commandment we have from him: whoever loves God must love his brother. (1 John 4:20–21)

Find a church that teaches the truth, one where people are not ashamed to wear his name and learn to love it.

CHRIST SEES THE CHURCH AS HIS BRIDE

In Ephesians 5:22–33, Jesus, through the apostle Paul, speaks of how the relationship between husband and wife should be like his relationship with the church. He speaks about his love for the church and how he gave himself up for it. He speaks of "nourishing and cherishing the church and cleansing her with water by the word so that he might present it to himself a glorious church, not having spot, or wrinkle, or any such thing; but that it should be holy and without blemish." Jesus loves and takes care of his church. John the Baptist also described Jesus as a bridegroom, and the apostle Paul told the church at Corinth that he had "espoused them to one husband to present them as a chaste virgin" (2 Cor. 11:1–2). Finally, the apostle John depicts the triumphant church as a bride descending from heaven (Rev. 21:1–3). This imagery of a bride demonstrates Christ's love for the church and the value he places on it.

Jesus did not just give his life on the cross; he gives his life every day, not only in his death. He denied self, loved and gave. "For God so loved the world, that he gave his only begotten Son, that whosoever believeth in him should not perish, but have everlasting life" (John 3:16, KJV). In Philippians 2:6–9 Paul tells us that Jesus gave up his throne in heaven to come to earth and set up his kingdom.

On his way back from collecting money for the famine in Jerusalem, Paul stopped in Miletus and met the Ephesian Elders. He warned them about false teachers and told them to "feed the church of God which He purchased with His own blood" (Acts 20:28). Jesus purchased the church with his blood. That fact, in and of itself, should give us every ounce of certainty that the church is valuable to Christ and is a large part of God's plan for the salvation of humankind. He did and does all that for the church, and so many people say they want no part of it. They are very far from having the mind of Christ, and if they do not want to be part of the church, Christ will not want any part of them.

IT IS HIS KINGDOM ON EARTH

The Bible teaches that the church is God's kingdom on the earth. In Matthew 16:18, Jesus told his disciples that he would build his church, and then he says to them, "I will give you the keys of the kingdom of heaven, and whatever you bind on earth shall be bound in heaven" (Matt. 16:19). Jesus ties the church and kingdom together in these verses. He also preached about the kingdom and prayed that the kingdom would come on earth as it is in heaven (Matt. 6:10). He proclaimed, "The time is fulfilled, and the kingdom of God is at hand; repent and believe in the gospel" (Mark 4:11). Jesus mentions the mysteries of the kingdom of heaven in Matthew 13:11. He died to bring God's kingdom into the world. When questioned by Pilate about being a king, Jesus answered,

> My kingdom is not from this world. If my kingdom were from this world, my servants would have been fighting, that I might not be delivered over to the Jews. But my kingdom is not from the world.(John 18:36).

Then Pilate asked, "So you are a king?" Jesus replied,

> You say that I am a king. For this purpose, I was born, and for this purpose, I have come into the world—to bear witness to the truth. Everyone who is of the truth listens to my voice. (John 18:37)

Jesus left the kingdom with his disciples to keep it growing. "You are those who have stayed with me in my trials, and I assign to you, as my Father assigned to me, a kingdom" (Luke 22:28–29). He gave the keys to the kingdom to them (Matt. 16:18–19). Jesus encouraged his disciples again in Luke 12:32, when he said, "Fear not little flock, it is your Father's good pleasure to give you the kingdom." From the apostles, those keys go to the kingdom and are passed on to the church. The church is now responsible for the kingdom of God on the earth. It is now up to us to spread the gospel message. Paul says that God sent Christ to establish this church "so that through the church the manifold wisdom of God might be made known to the rulers and authorities in heavenly places" (Eph. 3:9–10). "The purpose of the church is to carry on with the spread of the gospel, to proclaim the manifold wisdom of God" (Herrick 2004). The Hebrew writer also understood what role the church plays with this calling of God. He said, "Wherefore we receiving a kingdom which cannot be moved, let us have grace, whereby we may serve God acceptably with reverence and godly fear" (Heb. 12:28, KJV).

Jesus explains in his mustard seed parable that the kingdom/church starts small but will become great (Matt. 13:31-32). He also teaches his apostles that if they "had the faith of a mustard seed, they could move mountains and nothing would be impossible for them" (Matt. 17:20). Can you believe that? Look at the mustard seed. "The mustard plant in Palestine was one that starts with a small seed but grows to be a large tree." The Greek word for it is,

> Σίναπι, *sinapi*,: mustard, the name of a plant which in oriental countries grows from a very small seed and attains to the height of a tree, 10 feet (3 m) and more; hence a very small quantity of a thing is likened to a mustard seed, and also a thing which grows to a remarkable size. (J. H. Thayer 1982, 575–576).
>
> Think about this question: What makes a seed powerful? Its size does not matter. It is what is inside. There is where the power is. There is where the germ grows. Therefore, the power of faith is not in size but is in the promise that faith holds. The promise is the heart and core of faith, like the germ in the seed," (Bitter 2010).

The promise of a Home in Heaven gives strength and life to faith and faith moves us. For what are we willing to fight? What challenges are we willing to take on? How important is the promise of a home in Heaven to us? How strong is our germ?

There is value in this kingdom of heaven. It is more valuable than anything is in this world. Jesus teaches the worth of the treasure with two parables, *The Hidden Treasure* (Matt. 13:44) and *The Pearl of Great Price* (Matt. 13:45–46). In both parables men found something that was worth giving up everything to have. The kingdom of heaven is similar. It is so valuable that many would even give their life for it. Peter and John, apostles of Christ, would risk their lives to continue preaching the gospel message of salvation through Christ. When the

Jewish officials threatened to imprison them if they continued to teach that Jesus was the son of God, they said, "Whether it is right in the sight of God to listen to you rather than to God, you must judge, for we cannot but speak of what we have seen and heard" (Acts 4:19–20). We should remember that these two men were eyewitnesses to all the things that Jesus did. They knew he had died on the cross and they saw him after God raised him from the dead. They saw him lifted into heaven, and they heard the two angels tell them that he would return one day just like he left. There was no doubt in them that Jesus was the son of God and that he would fulfill his promises (Acts 1:11). The apostle Paul gave up all that he had gained as a Pharisee and counted it as a loss for the sake of Christ (Phil. 3:7–8). Do we have the kind of commitment that Jesus asks of us? Is the kingdom of heaven worth sacrificing to get?

CHAPTER SIX QUESTIONS

1. How are Christians supposed to think? (Phil. 1:2–5)
2. If Christ intimately aligns himself with the church, what should we do?
3. According to George Barna, "A biblical worldview is a way of dealing with the world such that we act like _____ twenty-four hours a day because we _____ like Jesus."
4. Describe Christ's view of the church as given by the apostle Paul in Ephesians 5:22–23.
5. Do you have the mind of Christ? If so, you have to _____ the church.
6. What does John say about loving the church? (1 John 4:20–21).
7. One cannot love Christ without _____ his church also.
8. Would you deny Christ His Bride, whom he purchased with his own blood? Yes/No
9. If Christ is a king, where is his kingdom?
10. What parable did Jesus offer to teach how fast the kingdom would grow?
11. What makes a seed powerful?
12. What two parables did Jesus teach to show the value of the kingdom?

SEVEN

Inside Forces That Hurt The Church

WHY IS THE HOUSE OF THE LORD FORSAKEN? NEHEMIAH 13

Nehemiah was a Jewish prophet held as a captive in Babylon during the Babylonian exile of the Jews in about 440 BC. Artaxerxes was the king of Babylon at this time. He allowed Nehemiah to go back to Jerusalem to find out why they were not working on restoring the wall and city. When Nehemiah reached Jerusalem, he found the wall still not complete and the city in disarray. He set out to find out why the house of the Lord had been forsaken.

Today God's house is the church. Paul said, "If I delay, you may know how one ought to behave in the household of God, which is the church of the living God a pillar and buttress of the truth" (1 Tim. 3:15). However, sometimes God's children can still forsake his house. Why?

One reason the house of the Lord was not finished was ignorance of the law. They were letting Ammonites and Moabites into their assemblies when the law said that they should never do that, but when they heard Nehemiah read the Law, they sent the entire group of foreigners away. They just did not know the law. People who go to church hear the law of Christ taught and preached, and they know to read and study their Bible every day, but many still do not study and they grow weaker and often leave.

Another reason the house of the Lord is forsaken is that its members do not separate from the world (Neh. 1:1–3). The Jews were supposed to separate from the foreigners. Christians today are supposed to be distinctive. "Do not be unequally yoked with unbelievers. For what partnership has righteousness with lawlessness, or what fellowship has light with darkness?" (2 Cor. 6:14). Paul told the Roman church to "be not conformed to the world, but be transformed by the renewing of your mind" (Rom. 12:2); John also told his readers,

> Do not love the world or the things in the world. If anyone loves the world, the love of the Father is not in him. For all that is in the world—the desires of the flesh and the desires of the eyes and pride of life—is not from the Father but is from the world. And the world is passing away along with its desires, but whoever does the will of God abides forever. (1 John 2:15–17)

Some Christians are too worldly, and that passion for worldly things often draws them away. Many people have jobs that require them to work on Sunday. That is a tough situation, but Jesus says,

> Whoever loves father or mother more than me is not worthy of me, and whoever loves son or daughter more than me is not worthy of me, and whoever does not take his cross and follow me is not worthy of me. Whoever finds his life will lose it, and whoever loses his life for my sake will find it. (Matt. 10:37–39).

A committed Christian would need to look for another job. Certainly, if one cannot even put his family before Christ, he cannot put his job before Christ. Missing church for work could cause the Christian to miss so much that he does not grow spiritually and he falls away, costing him his soul and hurting the cause of Christ in the world. It is better to lose a job than to lose your soul.

A fourth reason that people forsake the Lord's House is that some church members, and even church leaders live sinful lives. The leaders in Nehemiah's day were dishonest and easily bought. Christians must be clean in their thinking and their actions. Paul wrote, "Finally, brothers, whatever is true, whatever is honorable, whatever is just, whatever is pure, whatever is lovely, whatever is commendable if there be any excellence, if there is anything worthy of praise, think about these things" (Phil. 4:8). Paul told Timothy to "take no part in the sins of others, and keep yourself pure." This is something most people do not think about, but if you help someone who is sinning, you also sin. Paul, writing to the church in Ephesus, says,

> Let no one deceive you with empty words, for because of these things the wrath of God comes upon the sons of disobedience. Therefore do not become partners with them. (Eph. 5:6–7)

Paul continues by saying, "Take no part in the unfruitful works of darkness, but instead expose them. For it is shameful even to speak of the things that they do in secret" (vv. 11–12). The apostle John told his readers the same thing,

> Everyone who goes on ahead and does not abide in the teaching of Christ, does not have God. Whoever abides in the teaching has both the Father and the Son. If anyone comes to you and does not bring this teaching, do not receive him into your house or give him any greeting, for whoever greets him takes part in his wicked works. (2 John 1:9–11)

The law of the land today is the same. If you help someone commit a crime in any way, you are also charged. Churches need good, honest leaders and church members.

Greed and covetousness also hurts the church. When members do not contribute to the work of the church, the church is unable to support itself and do the things Christ needs them to do. In Nehemiah's day, he took steps to make sure they paid their tithes. The New Testament command is to "give as you have prospered" (1 Cor. 16:2), and "as you purpose in your heart" (2 Cor.9:7). In addition, verse 6 warns, "The point is this: whoever sows sparingly will also reap sparingly, and whoever sows bountifully will also reap bountifully." It hurts the church when its members do not give, and when you hurt the church, you hurt Christ ("Why are you persecuting me?" Acts 9:4–5; Matt. 25:31–46).

The Lord's Day is a special day of the week. In the Old Testament, the Sabbath Day was to be a holy day unto the Lord. There was to be no work done on that day. "Six days work shall be done, but on the seventh day, you shall have a Sabbath of solemn rest, holy to the Lord. Whoever does any work on it shall be put to death" (Exod. 35:2).

Christians are also to honor the Lord's Day as a holy day. "On the first day of the week, when we were gathered together to break bread, Paul talked with them, intending to depart on the next day, and he prolonged his speech until midnight" (Act 20:7). On the first day of the week, New Testament churches meet to commune with each other and the Lord and to worship the Lord. Jesus told his disciples that they were to do this "In remembrance of me" (Luke 22:19). Every Sunday we are to do that, so it cannot be just an ordinary day. When many members treat Sunday as any other day and do other things that keep them away, it hurts the church, and if it hurts the church, it hurts Christ.

In Nehemiah's day, the Israelites married women of other nations, which God told them not to do, and they had children who were born of these foreign women. God's reason for this law was that the foreign women worshipped idols and would pull their husbands away from following the true God to their idol worship. This also happens in the church today. Christians select a mate who is not Christian and, unless the Christian is strong enough, the mate may pull them down. This situation can also hurt their children's spiritual growth. When a mother attends and the father does not, the young boy may want to stay home with the father. This situation hurts the church, and if it hurts the church, it hurts Christ.

Jesus needs his disciples to carry out his great commission. That great commission calls the church to go out and make disciples,

> And Jesus came and said to them, "All authority in heaven and on earth has been given to me. Go therefore and make disciples of all nations, baptizing them in the name of the Father and of the Son and the Holy Spirit, teaching them to observe all that I have commanded you. And behold, I am with you always, even to the end of the age." (Matt. 28:18–20)

Jesus called the church to the cross to die, but other voices tempt us to do as we please. However, Jesus answers this dilemma in Luke 9:23b–24,

> ...for whoever would save his life will lose it, but whoever loses his life for my sake will save it. If anyone would come after me, let him deny himself and take up his cross daily and follow me.

The world teaches self-esteem; Christ teaches that self-denial, duty, loyalty, commitment, dedication, and sacrifice make disciples. (Hodge 2000, 77–78)

The church needs true disciples and without them, it suffers. And if the church suffers, Christ suffers.

When we stay away from the church, we hurt the church; we hurt Christ and his cause. We discourage those who are supposed to be our brothers and sisters. This causes them to leave, and then the church dies, which gravely hurts Christ.

LACKADAISICAL

My dad used a term for me when I first started playing baseball. He said I was too "lacksidaisical" [sic]. That is right, he would put the "s" in the middle of it, which this spell checker is having a hard time with. He was the team manager, but when he really got mad at me, he would call me just plain lazy, then he would make me run laps. By summer's end, I had named every blade of grass around the outfield, but I turned out to be a good baseball player. I still miss my dad.

Back to lackadaisical. It actually means "lazy, lacking spirit, halfhearted" (Tinkler 1996). I think that too many of us in the church have become lackadaisical in our spiritual lives. Where is the excitement and joy? There can be nothing in the world that inspires us more than God's love for us. John says, "We love because he first loved us" (1 John 4:19). John knew God's love first hand, and he tells us, "By this, we know love that he laid down his life for us, and we ought to lay down our lives for the brothers" (1 John 3:16).

Excitement and joy come when one sees a person come up from that watery grave, as a newborn Christian taking the first steps toward heaven. Excitement and joy come when you teach someone about Jesus, and they believe what you have taught and asks the question the eunuch asked Philip in the desert, "Here is water, what keeps me from being baptized?" (Acts 8:36)

What joy and excitement that brings. It also encourages the whole congregation and even the angels in heaven to rejoice. "Just so, I tell you, there will be more joy in heaven over one sinner who repents than over ninety-nine righteous persons who need no repentance" (Luke 15:7).

We have become lackadaisical in our worship. There is no spirit. Paul says to us, "For we are the circumcision, who worship by the Spirit of God and glory in Christ Jesus and put no confidence in the flesh" (Phil. 3:3). Worship should be a memorial to God and memorable to us.

We have become lackadaisical in our commitment to Christ. Some people come to services only and do nothing else in their life for the Lord. Each week has 168 hours and if you attend four services of one hour each, that is 4 hours, which means you are only at church 2.3% of your week. One would hope we would be studying, praying, teaching someone, and/or doing well for someone with much more of our time. This demonstrates the wrong motivation and wrong priorities. We do what we have to do, but in reality, we do not even do that. How many have you influenced for God this week? How many hours have you spent studying the Bible? How many hours have you been in prayer? Are you content with that?

EXCITEMENT

The church needs to get past the lackadaisical attitude and become excited about its mission because its mission is extremely important for the whole world. The church needs some exciting positive sermons to uplift everyone. We get excited about sports, hobbies, and business, but we should be in the clouds with excitement for our salvation. To sell a product, you must believe in it and be enthusiastic. If the church is going to sell salvation to anyone, it needs to believe in its own salvation.

Remember the excitement of the apostles. Peter and John had to go before the Jewish Sanhedrin, who told them not to preach anymore about Jesus. They said, "Whether it is right in the sight of God to listen to you rather than to God, you must judge, for we cannot but speak of what we have seen and heard" (Acts 4:19b–20). They went out preaching again and were arrested again. This time, they bravely told the Jewish officials that they "'Must obey God rather than man' (5:29). Then they left the presence of the council, rejoicing that they were counted worthy to suffer dishonor for the name" (Acts 5:41). They rejoiced in the privilege of suffering for Christ. Luke tells us that the people of Samaria felt much joy when they obeyed the gospel (8:8). Then we read about Paul and Silas singing while in the Philippian jail. Paul says that we should, "Rejoice in the Lord always" (Phil. 4:4). The Bible is a message of joy. Christians should rejoice because:

> Blessed be the God and Father of our Lord Jesus Christ!
> According to his great mercy, he has caused us to be

born again to a living hope through the resurrection of Jesus Christ from the dead, to an inheritance that is imperishable, undefiled, and unfading, kept in heaven for you, who by God's power are being guarded through faith for a salvation ready to be revealed in the last time. In this you rejoice, though now for a little while, if necessary, you have been grieved by various trials. (1 Pet. 1:3–6)

There are many reasons for joy in the Bible. There is the joy of a clear conscience, the joy of forgiveness, and the joy of a great burden removed (1 John 1:7). Paul was a murderer, but even his burden was taken away (1 Tim. 1:15). He said, "This is a faithful saying, and worthy of all acceptation, that Christ Jesus came into the world to save sinners; of whom I am chief" (1 Tim. 1:15, KJV). Think about King David's burden. He was an adulterer, a liar, and a murderer, and he prayed for forgiveness, "Restore to me the joy of your salvation and uphold me with a willing spirit" (Ps. 51:12).

There is also the joy of Christian fellowship. Christians are never alone; "the grace of the Lord Jesus Christ and the love of God and the fellowship of the Holy Spirit be with you all" (2 Cor. 13:14).

Then there is the joy of pleasing the Father, which comes from a deep conviction that "God is and is a rewarder of them that diligently seek him" (Heb. 11:6).

What does God do when someone neglects the church? First, if we stop working for God, he may stop working for us.

> Behold, the Lord's hand is not shortened, that it cannot save, or his ear dull, that it cannot hear, but your iniquities have made a separation between you and your God, and your sins have hidden his face from you so that he does not hear. (Isa. 59:1–2)

The purpose of God's discipline is to move us to fulfill our purpose in him and to support his saving work in the world. It has a loving purpose and brings all Christians to the highest good (Heb. 12:5–6). The church tries to teach the person and help them overcome their delinquency. If sin is involved, the person would need to confess and seek forgiveness, and the Lord will forgive them. Jesus died on the cross to redeem and rescue his people. He will restore you as you turn to him in repentance. "If we confess our sins, he is faithful and just to forgive us our sins and to cleanse us from all unrighteousness" (1 John 1:9).

Consider your ways, Christians; give careful thought to how you can involve yourselves in God's work. It must be the first priority. Be deliberate and committed to getting it done.

> I hope to come to you soon, but I am writing these things to you so that, if I delay, you may know how one ought to behave in the household of God, which is the church of the living God, a pillar and buttress of the truth. (1 Tim. 3:14–15)

What steps should you take to get involved in building up the church?

STANDING IN THE BREACH

> And I sought for a man among them who should build up the wall and stand in the breach before me for the land, that I should not destroy it, but I found none. (Ezek. 22:30)

The ways of the world seem to be getting increasingly worse. The desire for fun, fame, and fortune is infectious. It pollutes society and pulls Christians down. The mayor of a large city stole some money from the city and my wife heard a woman say, "That's ok, everybody steals." I surely hope not everybody steals. Christians lose their zeal saying they cannot do this or that for the church and the Lord, but to gain the acceptance of worldly friends, they will do almost anything. More and more jobs are requiring Sunday work, which takes people away from worship services, as do sporting and entertainment events. We have this demand for tolerance, even from our government, that requires us to accept other religions as equal to Christianity, even if they have evil workings. Things used to be such that one could say they hate the sin but love the sinner, but now we must accept their religion as equal to Christianity without challenge. The church needs people with the courage to stand in the breach and stop enemies of God.

Some people say we should not judge and quote Matthew 7:1 to justify that belief. However, we need also to look at the context of that verse. Jesus does use the words, "Judge not," but he ends the verse with the words, "that you be not judged." Then he continues, "For with the judgment you pronounce you will be judged, and with the measure you use it will be measured to you" (v. 2). Jesus tells us to consider our own righteousness before we condemn someone else (see vv. 5–6). "You hypocrite, first take the log out of your own eye, and then you will see clearly to take the speck out of your brother's eye." We can only do that by judging their acts. Jesus also tells us, "Do not judge by appearances, but judge with right judgment" (John 7: 24). Jesus gives us the right to judge, (cf. Matt. 7:16, 20) but our judgment must be gentle and scriptural.

> Brothers, if anyone is caught in any transgression, you who are spiritual should restore him in a spirit of gentleness. Keep watch on yourself, lest you too be tempted. (Gal. 6:1)

Christianity itself is to blame for some of the problems of humanity. Christians have compromised for the irresponsible fake salvation that Paul warned Timothy to avoid. He said,

> For the time is coming when people will not endure sound teaching, but having itching ears they will accumulate for themselves teachers to suit their own passions and will turn away from listening to the truth and wander off into myths. (2 Tim. 4:3)

Who has the integrity and courage to stop it? Will God find one who will stand in the breach today?

In Ezekiel's day, no one would stand in the breach. In Ezekiel 7:1–4, the Lord threatens to punish them and he says "then they will know that I am the Lord." The Lord used that phrase twenty-five times in the book of Ezekiel. Verses 10–13 describe their sins as pride, violence, and wickedness. They have blown the trumpet and prepared everything, but none goes to battle (v. 14). Verse 17 tells of their fear, how their hands were feeble and their knees turned to water. In verses 26–27, God tells them that "they will be judged according to their way, and that they will know that I am the Lord."

In Chapter 13, the false prophets are condemned. "Woe to the foolish prophets who follow their own spirit, and have seen nothing!" (13:3). "You have not gone into the breaches, or built up a wall for the house of Israel that it might stand in the battle in the day of the Lord" (13:5).

Chapter 22 condemns the shedding of blood in Israel and Ezekiel says to declare the abominations of the city. Even their princes shed blood against their own father and mother. They despised the holy things of God and profaned Sabbaths. The men uncovered their father's nakedness and violated women. Again, in verses 15–16, God says, of the people, that they would know that he is the Lord and that he will scatter them among the nations, and in verse 20, God says, "He will gather them in the city and blow the fire of his wrath on them." In verse 22, the Lord says "you will know that I am the Lord; I have poured my wrath upon you." God continues to pour his wrath upon them, their prophets and princes were evil and violent, and the Lord continues to say, "You will know that I am the Lord." In verse 30, God says that he "sought a man among them who should build up the wall and stand in the breach before me for the land, that I should not destroy it, but I found none."

In Chapter 23, God says that Israel had forgotten him and catered to the world (vv. 35, 40, 49). Israel would not stand up for God and his ways.

Are we doing the same thing today? Have we lost all integrity, sincerity, and dedication in our pursuit of fun, fame, and fortune? Have we forgotten God? Does Jesus require less of us in these matters? Jesus said to all,

> If anyone would come after me, let him deny himself and take up his cross daily and follow me. For whoever would save his life will lose it, but whoever loses his life for my sake will save it. For what does it profit a man if he gains the whole world and loses or forfeits himself? For whoever is ashamed of me and of my words, of him will the Son of Man be ashamed when he comes in his glory and the glory of the Father and of the holy angels. (Luke 9:23–26)

"But since we belong to the day, let us be sober, having put on the breastplate of faith and love, and for a helmet the hope of salvation" (1 Thess. 5:8). Will we take up these things and fight for God with them? Will we put on the armor of God and fight with it to keep God's way growing in this world.

When the Son of Man comes, "will he find faith on the earth?"(Luke 18:8b). Will we have the courage, integrity, and dedication to abandon worldliness and stand in the breach for Christ? The time is now! It cannot wait!

> During the time of the twelve Caesars, the Roman army would conduct morning inspections. As the inspecting Centurion would come in front of each legionnaire, the soldier would strike with his right fist the armor breastplate that covered his heart. The armor had to be strongest there in order to protect the heart from the sword thrusts and from arrow strikes. As the soldier struck his armor, he would shout "*integritas*," which, in Latin means material wholeness, completeness, and entirety. The inspecting

Centurion would listen closely for this affirmation and for the ring that well-kept armor would give off. Satisfied that the armor was sound and that the soldier beneath it is protected, he would then move on to the next man.

At about the same time, the Praetorians or imperial bodyguard were ascending into power and influence; drawn from the best "politically correct" soldiers of the legions, they received the finest equipment and armor. They no longer had to shout "*integritas*" to signify that their armor was sound. Instead, as they struck their breastplate, they would shout "Hail Caesar," to signify that their heart belonged to the imperial personage—not to their unit—not to an institution—not to a code of ideals. They armored themselves to serve the cause of a single man.

A century passed and the rift between the legion and the imperial bodyguard and its excesses grew larger. To signify the difference between the two organizations, the legionnaire, upon striking his armor would no longer shout *integritas*, but instead would shout *integer*. Integer means undiminished—complete—perfect. It not only indicated that the armor was sound; it also indicated that the soldier wearing the armor was sound of character. He was complete in his integrity....his heart was in the right place...his standards and morals were high. He was not associated with the immoral conduct that was rapidly becoming the signature of the Praetorian Guards.

The armor of integrity continued to serve the legion well. For over four centuries they held the line against the marauding Goths and Vandals, but by 383 A.D., the social decline that infected the republic and the Praetorian Guard had its effects upon the legion.

As a 4th-century Roman general wrote, "When because of negligence and laziness, parade ground drills were abandoned, the customary armor began to feel heavy since the soldiers rarely, if ever, wore it. Therefore, they first asked the emperor to set aside the breastplates and mail and then the helmets. Therefore, our soldiers fought the Goths without any protection for the heart and head, and the Goths would often beat them with their archers. Although there were many disasters, which led to the loss of great cities, no one tried to restore the armor to the infantry. They took their armor off and when the armor came off—so too came their integrity." It was only a matter of a few years until the legion rotted from within and was unable to hold the frontiers. The barbarians were at the gates. (Frances 2002, 103–106)

The church needs soldiers who will wear God's armor and stand in the breach, warning his brothers and sisters about false teachers, trials, and temptations, and will fight the good fight (1 Tim.6:12; 2 Tim. 4:7).

CHAPTER SEVEN QUESTIONS

1. List seven problems that prevented the rebuilding of the wall in the first section of this chapter.
2. What things does Paul tell the church at Philippi to think about?
3. Define lackadaisical.
4. Can you say that God's love for you and sacrifice for you excite you? Yes/No
5. How do you feel when a clean soul comes up from that watery grave cleansed, saved, and ready to be used?
6. Do you remember what the Ethiopian Eunuch did? (Acts 8:39).
7. List the things we have in the church that brings joy?
8. Do you think it is right to stay away from worshiping God for a job, or an athletic event? Yes/No
9. What does standing in the breach of the wall have to do with anything?
10. What did God mean by "Then you will know that I am the Lord"?

EIGHT

Outside Forces That Hurt The Church

IGNORING GOD – GENESIS 25:19–34

Ignoring God is a terrible sin, and one who does this has an attitude that God is not necessary. Even though they may say the right spiritual things, if they live as though God does not exist, they condemn themselves. When we are not close to God, we act without thinking about him. Abraham had two important grandchildren, twin boys. Have you ever noticed that Jacob, the youngest, is always mentioned first (Josh. 24:4; Heb. 11:20)? Esau made a spontaneous choice one day in a field near a warm fire that showed his attitude toward God. This crucial flaw, forgetting God, often catches us unprepared too.

Isaac knew and believed the great truths about himself and his descendants (Gen. 12:1–2; 13:14–16; 18:16–19; 22:11–12, 15–18; 26:1–5). One would surely think Esau would know all this too. He also would know the inheritance benefits given to the firstborn. The firstborn son would be dedicated to God and receive a double portion of everything his father owned (Exod. 22:29; Deut. 21:17). In Genesis 27:18–29, when Isaac blessed Jacob thinking he was Esau, Jacob would receive physical blessings from the land, he would lord over nations, and he would receive protection from his enemies. Esau despised his birthright (Gen. 25:34), and since God gives the birthright, he despised God. The Hebrew writer warns that we should not be

> ...immoral or unholy like Esau, who sold his birthright for a single meal. For you know that afterward when he desired to inherit the blessing, he was rejected, for he found no chance to repent, though he sought it with tears. (Heb. 12:16–17)

Paul uses the words "ungodly" and "godless" (profane) when he speaks of the law.

> Knowing this, that the law is not made for a righteous man, but for the lawless and disobedient, for the ungodly and for sinners, for unholy and profane, for murderers of fathers and murderers of mothers, for manslayers, for whoremongers, for them that defile themselves with mankind, for men stealers, for liars, for perjured persons, and if there be any other thing that is contrary to sound doctrine. (1 Tim.1:9–10)

How does ungodliness manifest itself? One way is through the abuse of one's body with worldly things. God wants us to glorify him in our bodies (1 Cor. 6:19–20). We are meant to be a living sacrifice.

> Or do you not know that your body is a temple of the Holy Spirit within you, whom you have from God? You are not your own, for you were bought with a price. So glorify God in your body. (Rom. 12:1)

Hurting people with our tongues is another way the work of the church suffers in the world. We can cause great trouble for people and nations with our tongues. James warns us about the power to hurt that is in the tongue when he says,

> But no human being can tame the tongue. It is a restless evil, full of deadly poison. With it, we bless our Lord and Father, and with it, we curse people who are made in the likeness of God. From the same mouth, come blessing and cursing. My brothers, these things ought not to be so. (James 3:8–10)

These problems with the tongue contribute to the overall atmosphere in the world, which is antagonistic toward religion and the church. There is also so much profanity on the television, causing people and even children to think that it is ok to talk this way, and the way we talk is often the way we walk. The world seems to become more evil every day, and this affects the church.

A third thing that contributes to the way of the world and makes the church's mission more difficult is how we credit ourselves with our blessings. The Bible says, "Beware lest you say in your heart, 'My power and the might of my hand have gotten me this wealth'" (Deut. 8:17). People today think they can do it all themselves, that they do not need God, and this attitude makes the growth of the church difficult.

Another thing people of the world do to make church's growth difficult is seeking their own will rather than the will of God. They say, "Today or tomorrow we will go into such and such a town and spend a year there and trade and make a profit" (James 4:13). Jesus' example was to pray "My Father if it is possible, let this cup pass from me; nevertheless, not as I will but as you will" (Matt. 26:39).

Finally, people love themselves more than they do their neighbor or God. Selfish people will not care about the condition of their neighbor or their church. Paul predicted this,

> For people will be lovers of self, lovers of money, proud, arrogant, abusive, disobedient to their parents, ungrateful, unholy, heartless, unappeasable, slanderous, without self-control, brutal, not loving good, treacherous, reckless, swollen with conceit, lovers of pleasure rather than lovers of God, having

the appearance of godliness, but denying its power. Avoid such people. (2 Tim. 3:2–5)

He also says, "Know and love God, be strengthened by Him, bear fruit for him" (Col. 1:9–12). If people would listen to what he said here and follow it, the church would have a much easier time in the world.

POSTMODERNISM AND ITS EFFECTS ON THE CHURCH

Our culture has changed in ways that are hostile to Christianity and our way of life. There are three tenants to this new world philosophy. They are postmodernism, the new tolerance, and multiculturalism.

Postmodernism affects all aspects of our lives. It affects religion, education, history, science, literature, language, medicine, and psychology. It affects religion primarily because of its claim of no absolute truth (McCallum 1996, 48). Postmodernism does not allow for there to be an absolute truth, which contradicts Jesus' teaching. Jesus says, "and you will know the truth, and the truth will set you free" (John 8:32). Again, Jesus says, "I am the way, and the truth, and the life. No one comes to the Father except through me. If you had known me, you would have known my Father also. From now on you do know him and have seen him" (John 14:6–7). Postmodernism says that truth is relative, fixed by outside reality, and determined either culturally or individually. Absolute truth is truth that is objective, universal, and constant.

Some postmodernists say that

> All religions, including Christianity, is a myth; metaphors that reflect primal longings in the human psyche, and the psyche is the personal experience of our bodily functions – that is, our instincts drive the biological processes, fears, and conflicts. ... Once we see that every religion is simply a mythological

framework for self-discovery, all final distinctions between religions evaporate. (D. McCallum 1996, 218)

This philosophy makes us humans no more than animals. Postmodernism also affects the church with its philosophy concerning literature. Postmodernists have made literature reader-centered. They claim that the writer wrote with his cultural bias and we cannot recover that. This means the reader becomes the source and judge of a text's meaning, and the Bible is no exception. It also means that there is no absolute truth. Every man could make up whatever truth he wanted. It would be as it was in the book of Judges, "In those days there was no king in Israel. Everyone did what was right in his own eyes" (Judg. 21:25). That would lead to chaos.

Postmodernists say that history is cultural. Each culture is equal and we should not try to change another culture. This philosophy affects the church's ability to evangelize. If we decide to teach someone the gospel, we are trying to judge his or her culture, and that is discrimination. These philosophies make it more difficult to convince people that God is God and that the Bible is his word. "For no prophecy was ever produced by the will of man, but men spoke from God as they were carried along by the Holy Spirit" (2 Pet. 1:20–21).

THE NEW TOLERANCE

The new tolerance is another philosophy that makes the church's growth difficult. Helbock defines it as,

> Every individual's beliefs, values, lifestyles, and perception of truth claims are equal. ... There is no hierarchy of truth. All beliefs are equal, and all truth is relative. (1996, 2)

It bases its philosophy on the unbiblical belief that "truth is relative to the community in which a person participates, and since there are many human communities, by necessity, there are many truths"

(McDowell 1998, 18). The new tolerance claims that there can be no judgment of another's beliefs or behaviors. Their position is just as valid as ours and we must offer our sincere support to them, right or wrong.

MULTICULTURALISM

> Multiculturalism is an educational movement designed to facilitate awareness and appreciation of diverse cultures. In postmodern ideology, it teaches that cultures should be empowered to preserve, unchanged, their unique cultural reality. If one makes any effort to change or reform a cultural group it is seen as repression, domination, and colonizing of one group by another. (D. McCallum 1996, 282–283)

This philosophy eliminates evangelizing anyone. If we try to convert someone from a life of sin, we are belittling him and placing ourselves above him. Multiculturalism destroys the mandate given to the church by Jesus to teach the good news of salvation to the whole world (Matt. 28: 19–20). In addition, if allowed to take over completely, it would do away with the church and all of Christianity. However, many people through history have tried to eliminate the Bible, and it is still here with the best promise of all. No matter what postmodernists or anyone else does, the Bible is true. Its very existence in the world today proves that. God takes care of his word and his people. The message in his word is wonderful. "They will make war on the Lamb, and the Lamb will conquer them, for he is Lord of lords and King of kings, and those with him are called and chosen and faithful" (Rev. 17:14).

The postmodern movement may make it difficult for the church to carry on its mission to make known the manifold wisdom of God (Eph.3:10). Nevertheless, the church will get it done. Just as Peter and John said to the Jewish officials, the church today will say, "Whether it is right in the sight of God to listen to you rather than to God, you must judge, for we cannot but speak of what we have seen and heard" (Acts 4:18–20).

Dennis McCallum points out that,

> Christians are not here to offer the world a premier rapturous experience. We are here to declare the truth about Jesus Christ and call on sinful people to fall on their knees and repent—often an experience more painful than pleasurable. Jesus says when we are His disciples "the truth will set you free" (John 8:32). (1996, 249)

CHAPTER EIGHT QUESTIONS

1. What might happen when we ignore God?
2. List five ways that ungodliness manifests itself in the first section of this chapter.
3. What does postmodernism say about the truth?
4. What does Jesus say about the truth?
5. What do you think about the truth?
6. What does "They made literature reader-centered" mean?
7. What is the problem with the new tolerance?
8. Define multiculturalism.
9. What does it do to the church and all of Christianity?
10. What does Acts 20:28 tell church leaders to be aware of?
11. What happens to those who do not abide in the teaching of Christ? (2 John 1:7, 9–11)

NINE

Religious Division

BAPTISM

The Bible warns us about false teachers. We must guard against them. Paul warns the Ephesian elders about them,

> Pay careful attention to yourselves and to all the flock, in which the Holy Spirit has made you overseers, to care for the church of God, which he purchased with his own blood. I know that after my departure fierce wolves will come in among you, not sparing the flock; and from among your own selves will arise men speaking twisted things, to draw away the disciples after them. (Acts 20:28–30)

He warned the Galatians too,

> I am astonished that you are so quickly deserting him who called you in the grace of Christ and are turning to a different gospel, not that there is another one, but there are some who trouble you and want to distort the gospel of Christ. But even if we or an angel from

heaven should preach to you a gospel contrary to the one we preached to you, let him be accursed. (Gal 1:6–8)

He also warned the church at Thessalonica about false teachers,

> Let no one deceive you in any way. For that day will not come, unless the rebellion comes first, and the man of lawlessness is revealed, the son of destruction who opposes and exalts himself against every so-called god or object of worship, so that he takes his seat in the temple of God, proclaiming himself to be God. (2 Thess. 2:3–4)

John also warned his readers,

> Beloved, do not believe every spirit, but test the spirits to see whether they are from God, for many false prophets have gone out into the world. By this, you know the Spirit of God: every spirit that confesses that Jesus Christ has come in the flesh is from God and every spirit that does not confess Jesus is not from God. This is the spirit of the antichrist, which you heard was coming and now is in the world already. Little children, you are from God and have overcome them, for he who is in you is greater than he who is in the world. (1 John 4:1–4)

John warned them a second time,

> Everyone who goes on ahead and does not abide in the teaching of Christ does not have God. Whoever abides in the teaching has both the Father and the Son. If anyone comes to you and does not bring this teaching, do not receive him into your house or give him any greeting, for whoever greets him takes part in

his wicked works. For many deceivers have gone out into the world, those who do not confess the coming of Jesus Christ in the flesh. Such a one is the deceiver and the antichrist. (2 John 1:7, 9–11)

Paul warns the church at Ephesus again, "Let no one deceive you with empty words, for because of these things the wrath of God comes upon the sons of disobedience. Therefore do not become partners with them" (Eph. 5:6–7).

Those warnings are there for us today also. There are thousands–maybe millions–of false teachers in the world, and a whole bunch of them are in the United States. The most important and dangerous divisions are over the plan of salvation. It amazes me that common sense has left the planet. There are nine events in Acts that describe what people did to be saved and in every one the people were baptized. There are no other accounts of people in the act of being saved in the New Testament. The only other baptisms in the New Testament are those of John the Baptist, and they had to be re-baptized after the new covenant took effect when Jesus died on the cross. Paul re-baptized the twelve men in Ephesus who John the Baptist had baptized (Acts 19:1–5).

Baptism is as much a commandment as believing (something the person has to do) and repenting (again, something the person has to do). Can a person be saved before his sins are washed away? The apostle Paul could not (Acts 22:16). What about Cornelius and his household? The Bible says that Peter commanded them to be baptized. Why did the eunuch ask Philip if he could be baptized? He asked because Philip taught him that he needed to be baptized. Many people want to bring up the thief on the cross. But the thief on the cross lived and died under the old Law of Moses. Both he and Jesus lived under that law. Christ's will, which required one to be baptized, did not take effect until after Christ died (Heb. 9:15–17).

Do you think God would have been pleased with Abraham if he had not offered Isaac as a sacrifice? Do you think Christ would have kept the same apostles had they refused to go to all nations, teaching and baptizing? Jesus told them to do it! Is he Lord or not? Baptism is a work of faith that Jesus commands, and the magic that takes place when one comes up out of that water is the scratching on the paper as God writes his name in the Book of Life. Those who teach that baptism is not needed for salvation are false teachers. They are causing many sincere people to lose their soul.

Nowhere does the Bible tell us to pray to be saved. You might pray to God to show you the way, and if you have the right heart, he will providentially arrange for someone to teach you the way. One must have his sins washed away to be saved. "Indeed, under the law, almost everything is purified with blood, and without the shedding of blood, there is no forgiveness of sins" (Heb. 9:22). Baptism is where we come in contact with the blood and our sins are washed away (Acts 22:16). The conversion of Cornelius and his house is an example that praying is not enough to get us into the kingdom of God (Acts 10:1ff). Cornelius, a Roman centurion, was a devout man who feared God with his entire house and prayed always, but it did not save him. God heard his prayers and sent an angel, but the angel did not teach him. The angel told Cornelius to send for Peter. It had to be a human who would bring the message of salvation to him because that was the plan Jesus created with his apostles when he gave them the key to the kingdom. God planned it that way before the beginning of the world. Jesus wanted his disciples to use the key to the kingdom he gave to them (Matt. 16:16–19). The key to the kingdom was not a literal key. Jesus used the word "key" symbolically. The real key was Peter's confession that Jesus was the Christ, the son of God, who would bring salvation to the world. That gospel message is the key. The apostles would teach others to do the same and open the door to the kingdom of God. Therefore, Peter came and taught Cornelius and his household, and in the end, he commanded them to be baptized (Acts 10:48). They obeyed that command the same night. One should not miss that word "commanded" in this verse. Peter did not say, "If you want to." He did not say it was optional; he commanded him to be baptized in the name of (by the authority of) Jesus Christ.

Another example is in Acts chapter 2; the people asked Peter what they must do. Peter answered, "Repent and be baptized for the remission of your sins." Three thousand souls did so that day, and the Lord added the saved to the church. Jesus did not add them to the church before they were baptized, only after. In addition, Philip must have taught the Ethiopian eunuch about baptism because the man stopped his chariot and said, "Here is water, what prevents me from being baptized?" Philip answered, "If you believe you may," and they went down into the water and the man was baptized, and he went on his way rejoicing. The eunuch did not rejoice before he was baptized (Acts 8:26–39, ASV). He rejoiced after his baptism.

The baptism process is just like Abraham's situation when God ordered him to sacrifice Isaac (Gen. 22:2–18). If Abraham had not been willing to make the sacrifice, we would not have called him the father of the faithful. His faith in God moved him to trust that God would do what he promised. His willingness to offer Isaac was an act of faith. God would not have been pleased with Abraham if he had not done what he commanded him to do. Baptism is also an act of faith. When a person believes with all his heart and is willing to repent (change his life and follow Jesus), then baptism is that work of faith that washes away sin and demonstrates their faith. Paul tells the church at Thessalonica that he "remembered their work of faith." Baptism is a work of faith (1 Thess. 1:3). The salvation process is hear the word, believe the word (John 8:24), repent (Acts 17:30), confess your belief (Rom. 10: 9–10), and be baptized (Matt. 28:19–20; Mark 16:15–16; Gal. 3:25–27). To wash away your sins is the process for membership in the church and a place in heaven.

Martin Luther's doctrine of "saved by faith alone" has caused some people to think that all they have to do is believe and they will be saved and can live any way they want.

Martin Luther (1483–1546) was a German priest who did not like the Catholic church's selling of indulgences (reduces the punishment for sin) for money or property or anything of value. Therefore, a person could pay a sum of money and sin without any guilt or worry because he had already paid for it. Luther was right; indulgence was very sinful.

However, in reaction to it, he went too far in the other direction. He studied and developed a theory that faith was all that was necessary for Jesus to save us, with no work needed. He even went as far as to add the word "alone" after the word "faith" in Romans 5:1 even though it was not in any of the manuscripts. The only place the words "faith" and "alone" are together in the New Testament is in James 2:24, "You see that a person is justified by works and not by faith alone." Note, "Not by faith alone."

It is true that the "faith only" doctrine took value away from the indulgences, but it also caused some other problems. Some of those who believe that faith alone saves take that doctrine to heart and do not repent (change their lives) or even stop any sinful actions. Their lives just go on as if all those sinful things are ok and they think they are saved because they claim to have faith.

What is faith? Whatever it is, we must have it. The Hebrew writer defines faith as "assurance, (conviction), and evidence (proof) of things not seen" (11:1). He also tells us that we must have faith. "And without faith, it is impossible to please him, for whoever would draw near to God must believe that he exists and that he rewards those who seek him" (Heb. 11:6).

Real faith transforms one's entire existence. It transformed the Pharisee Saul into the Apostle Paul who said:

> For to me to live is Christ, and to die is gain. If I am to live in the flesh, that means fruitful labor for me. Yet which I shall choose I cannot tell. I am hard pressed between the two. My desire is to depart and be with Christ, for that is far better. But to remain in the flesh is more necessary on your account. (Phil.1:21–24)

Faith is like running from a fire in a burning field and you come to a cliff where you cannot see what is below. Suddenly, you hear a voice yell, "Jump, I can catch you." You say, "I can't see you." The voice yells again, "Jump, I can see you." The voice is the evidence, the proof that someone is waiting to catch you. What will you do, die in the fire or jump? There is enough evidence on this earth to have faith in God. This great creation is one proof (Rom. 1:21–22) and God's word, the Bible, is another. Will you trust God and jump into his waiting arms and be saved or will you die in the fire?

The apostle Paul says that it is easy to find faith, "So faith comes from hearing, and hearing through the word of God" (Rom. 10:17). Paul also instructed Timothy to trust the scripture,

> …and how from childhood you have been acquainted with the sacred writings, which are able to make you wise for salvation through faith in Christ Jesus. All Scripture is breathed out by God and profitable for teaching, for reproof, for correction, and for training in righteousness, that the man of God may be complete, equipped for every good work. (2 Tim. 3:15–17)

Again, the Bible is the voice, the evidence. It has everything you need, it teaches you what to do to be saved, it is good for teaching, reproof, correction, and training. It helps one become complete in everything one needs. You cannot get any more complete than complete. You cannot be any more perfect than perfect. So all you need is your Bible.

Faith is more than belief. It involves trust and action. Faith in Christ transforms our effect, motives, thoughts, hopes, and our entire life. Wolfhart Pannenberg, a German theologian (1928–2014), explains faith as "The evidence for Jesus' resurrection is so strong that nobody would question it except for two things: First, it is a very unusual event. And second, if you believe it happened, you have to change the way you live" (2009, n.p.) "However, if we walk in the light, as he is in the light, we have fellowship with one another, and the blood of Jesus his Son cleanses us from all sin" (1 John 1:7). "Therefore, if anyone is in Christ, he is a new creation. The old has passed away; behold, the new has come" (2 Cor.5:17).

You have to make the jump into the waiting arms. Real faith produces obedience to prove it is real. Real faith gives courage and confidence. David and Goliath; Daniel, Shadrach, Meshach, and Abednego; Joseph; Peter, and John (Acts 4) all had great faith and stood up for God and remained faithful even when facing death. Faith gives us freedom and peace. Take the jump; it is worth it. It includes a willingness to repent, to change your life. "The times of ignorance God overlooked, but now he commands all people everywhere to repent" (Acts 17:30). It includes confessing your belief. "Also I say unto you, whosoever shall confess me before men, he shall the Son of man also confess before the angels of God" (Luke 12:8) and it includes baptism. "He said to them, 'Go into all the world and proclaim the gospel to the whole creation. Whoever believes and is baptized will be saved, but whoever does not believe will be condemned'" (Mark 16:15–16). "Baptism, which corresponds to this, now saves you, not as a removal of dirt from the body but as an appeal to God for a good conscience, through the resurrection of Jesus Christ"(1 Pet. 3:21) (Acts 2:38; Acts 22:16).

ONCE SAVED ALWAYS SAVED

Once saved, always saved is another doctrine that divides and is propagated by false teachers.

This is simple. "You are severed from Christ, you who would be justified by the law; you have fallen away from grace" (Gal. 5:4). The apostle Paul sure thought he could fall from grace. "But I keep under my body, and bring it into subjection: lest that by any means when I have preached to others, I myself should be a castaway" (1 Cor. 9:27, KJV). "Remember therefore from where you have fallen; repent, and do the works you did at first. If not, I will come to you and remove your lampstand from its place, unless you repent" (Rev. 2:5).

CHAPTER NINE QUESTIONS

1. Paul warns the Ephesian Elders about _____.
2. Paul warns the Galatians about _____.
3. Paul warns the Thessalonians about _____.
4. Who also gets punished in 2 John 1:7–9? (Eph. 5:6–7)
5. Did Jesus command his apostles to go and make disciples, baptizing them in the name of the Father, Son, and Holy Spirit, and teaching them all things that I have taught you? (Matt. 28:19–20)
6. Can anyone refuse to follow a command of Jesus and please him? Yes/No
7. How many examples of people being saved are there in the Acts? How many of them were baptized?
8. How does one get faith?
9. Real faith moves one to _____.
10. There is no place in the Bible that says God will save you by praying. Yes/No
11. Was Cornelius saved by prayer or by Peter coming to teach him?
12. Baptism is essential for salvation. Yes/No

TEN

What Makes A Strong Church?

Some first-century churches were strengthened in faith and they increased in numbers daily (Acts 16:5), but others were not as strong. Since the cause is so great, the church has to get strong. After all, our enemies are the rulers, the authorities, the cosmic powers over this present darkness, and the spiritual forces of evil in the heavenly places (Eph. 6:12).

Even so, God has given us the equipment we need to win this battle.

> The belt of truth, the breastplate of righteousness, shoes for your feet, for the readiness given by the gospel of peace. He has given us the shield of faith, to extinguish all the flaming darts of the evil one; the helmet of salvation, the sword of the Spirit, which is the word of God, and prayer. To that end keep alert with all perseverance. (Eph. 6:14–18)

All we have to provide is a proper mindset. Remember, have this mind in you (Phil. 2:5). That is what God called us to do. To have God in our mind. To know God. When Jesus prayed for his disciples in John 17, he asked his Father to grant them eternal life and to allow them to know him, the one true God and Jesus Christ whom he sent. The knowledge of God brings great blessings to our lives; joy, peace, and contentment. The Lord says, through Jeremiah the prophet,

> Let not the wise man boast in his wisdom, let not the mighty man boast in his might, let not the rich man boast in his riches, but let him who boasts boast in this, that he understands and knows me, that I am the LORD who practices steadfast love, justice, and righteousness in the earth. For in these things, I delight. (9:23–24)

To be a good church, the members need to know God intimately. They need to have a close relationship with him, and their minds must be focused on their spiritual strength, not strength as the world sees it. Some things may be present in the world to make us think we have a good relationship with God, but they are not guarantees. Jesus said, "Not everyone who says to me, 'Lord, Lord,' will enter the kingdom of heaven, but the one who does the will of my Father who is in heaven" (Matt 7:21). For instance, a congregation may have a large membership, but that does not mean it has the right mindset. The Lord said to the nation of Israel,

> It was not because you were more in number than any other people that the Lord set his love on you and chose you, for you were the fewest of all peoples, but it is because the Lord loves you and is keeping the oath that he swore to your fathers. (Deut. 7:7–8)

Jesus also warns us about following the crowd when He said, "Enter by the narrow gate. For the gate is wide and the way is easy that leads to destruction, and those who enter by it are many. For the gate is narrow and the way is hard that leads to life, and those who find it are few" (Matt. 7:13–14). The majority is not necessarily safe. You may have wealth, education, popularity, or honor among men, but it does not mean your relationship with God is right. Paul warns us,

> Consider your calling, brothers: not many of you were wise according to worldly standards, not many were powerful, not many were of noble birth. But God chose what is foolish in the world to shame the wise; God chose what is weak in the world to shame the strong; God chose what is low and despised in the world, even things that are not, to bring to nothing things that are, so that no human being might boast in the presence of God. (1 Cor. 1:26–29)

For the church to be vibrant, each member must be truly converted, not merely whitewashed. Jesus says, "Truly, I say to you, unless you turn and become like children, you will never enter the kingdom of heaven" (Matt.18:3). Luke, led by the Holy Spirit, tells us, "Repent, therefore and turn back, that your sins may be blotted out" (Acts 3:19). Paul tells the church in Rome,

> I appeal to you, therefore, brothers, by the mercies of God, to present your bodies as a living sacrifice, holy and acceptable to God, which is your spiritual worship. Do not be conformed to this world, but be transformed by the renewal of your mind, that by testing you may discern what the will of God is, what is good and acceptable and perfect. (Rom. 12:1–2)

When we renew our mind we will change our actions. We will walk in newness of life.

> Do you not know that all of us who have been baptized into Christ Jesus were baptized into his death? We were buried therefore with him by baptism into death, so that, just as Christ was raised from the dead by the

glory of the Father, we too might walk in newness of life. (Rom. 6:3–4)

We will be new creatures, the old person of sin will be gone, and we will follow Christ.

Not only will we follow him, but we will be zealous for his cause: "For the love of Christ controls us, because we have concluded this: that one has died for all…" (2 Cor. 5:14). The Greek word for "control" in this passage is συνέχω (sunechō); it means to hold together, that is, to compress, figuratively to compel, constrain, hold (Thayer 1982, 604). It is a strong word that demonstrates the power of the love Christ has to influence us to follow and do the things he would have us to do. His love both constrains us and compels us. It constrains us because we want to please him, so we follow and obey him and it compels us, driving us on to serve his cause.

Paul instructs the Roman Church to "not be slothful in zeal, be fervent in spirit, and serve the Lord" (Rom. 12:11). Paul taught the same to the Church at Corinth. "Therefore, my beloved brothers, be steadfast, immovable, always abounding in the work of the Lord, knowing that in the Lord your labor is not in vain" (1 Cor. 15:58). The apostle Peter taught the same thing in 2 Peter 1:5–11 and used the word "diligent" in verses 5 and 10. To be a vibrant church, its members must be diligent in their service to God and their fellow man.

To be an active church, its members need to be students of God's word. Paul instructed Timothy to "Do your best to present yourself to God as one approved, a worker who does not need to be ashamed, rightly handling the word of truth" (2 Tim. 2:15). Jesus said that those who hunger and thirst for righteousness are blessed and will be satisfied. The Psalmist says, "His delight is in the law of the LORD, and on his law, he meditates day and night" (Ps. 1:2). Peter says, "Like newborn infants, long for the pure spiritual milk, that by it you may grow up into salvation" (2 Pet.2:2). In his list of virtues, Peter commanded his readers to add to their faith with virtue and with virtue knowledge (2 Pet. 1:5). A church also needs good preaching from God's word (2 Tim. 4:2). In this verse, Paul tells Timothy to preach the word, be ready in season and out of season, reprove, rebuke, and exhort, with complete patience and teaching.

To have a faithful church, each member must be rich in faith. Romans 10:17 tells us that "faith comes from hearing, and hearing through the word of Christ." Faith is the absolute thing that members of the church need because it is the center of trusting God and without it, one cannot please God (Heb. 11:6). Faith must be proven by actions (James 2:17). Genuine faith is what moves one to follow Jesus and do the things he wants us to do. It is the thing that motivates Christians to obey his commandments, to attend the church gatherings, live a righteous life, and evangelize the world. First-century Christians met on the first day of the week, which is Sunday (Acts 20:7), but out of their newfound zeal, they also met every day in the temple and in houses, and they ceased not to teach (Acts 5:42). Their instructions were not to forsake the assembly (remember Hebrews 10:25). They needed to know more about God's plans, so they could execute them properly. How were they going to build up one another and move one another to love and do good works if they were not present to do those things? Those works would help spread the message and save their souls.

A strong church needs to be unified. Paul said to the church in Corinth,

> I appeal to you, brothers, by the name of our Lord Jesus Christ, that all of you agree, and that there be no divisions among you, but that you be united in the same mind and the same judgment. For it has been reported to me by Chloe's people that there is quarreling among you, my brothers. What I mean is that each one of you says, "I follow Paul," or "I follow Apollos," or "I follow Cephas," or "I follow Christ." Is Christ divided? Was Paul crucified for you? Or were you baptized in the name of Paul? (1 Cor.1:10–13)

In addition, there is Jesus' prayer in John 17. He prayed for his apostles to be able to carry on with his message. He asked for blessings for them, He also prayed for all his followers:

> ...that they may all be one, just as you, Father, are in me, and I in you, that they also may be in us, so that the world may believe that you have sent me. The glory that you have given me I have given to them, that they may be one even as we are one, I in them and you in me, that they may become perfectly one, so that the world may know that you sent me and loved them even as you loved me. (John 17:21–23)

Boy! We messed that one up, didn't we? Yes, we did and we have kept it messed up for at least the last 500 years. It started when all of the reformers decided to leave the Catholic Church. It was a great thing to do, but there was no unification and they splintered into many different denominations with different leaders who developed doctrines that were not, and still cannot be found in the Bible. In reaction to the Catholic chokehold, the stiff penalties, and suffering that they caused, the Reformers went too far in the other direction with doctrines that turned us almost completely loose. The problem is that they let Satan loose too. Now, in this country, it is getting very close to every man can do what is right in his own eyes (Deut. 12:8). "The way of a fool is right in his own eyes, but a wise man listens to advice" (Prov. 12:15). To be a strong church, we need unity, and not just within local congregations but in the entire worldwide church. Straight is the gate and narrow the way (Matt.7:13).

To have a good church, we need efficient, effective leadership. In the Old Testament, as went the leaders so went the nation (cf. Acts 20:28–32). The apostle Paul told Timothy, "What you have heard from me in the presence of many witnesses entrust to faithful men who will be able to teach others also" (2 Tim. 2:2). Paul also teaches Timothy, "The saying is trustworthy: If anyone aspires to the office of overseer, he desires a noble task" (1 Tim.3:1). He further says, "Let the elders who rule well be considered worthy of double honor, especially those who labor in preaching and teaching" (1 Tim. 5:17). The titles, bishop, overseer, elder, and pastor are all different titles for the same office (Acts 20:17–30). Verse 17 says that he called for the elders and in verse 28, he acknowledges that they are overseers and charges them to feed the flock, which is the actions of a pastor. So, whether you call them elder, pastor, or bishop, it does not matter; they are the same and there is never just one in a local church. Every time they are mentioned in the New Testament, it is always plural. Preachers are not elders or pastors or bishops unless the congregation makes them one and then he can only be one if there is already another one or more, or at least another one taking office at the same time.

One can find the qualifications for this position in 1 Timothy 3:1–7 and Titus 2:5–9. That brings us to one of the problems I mentioned above about men teaching doctrines that are not in the Bible or forbidden completely. For instance, some in today's world think it is perfectly fine for women to preach and teach religious things to men and that they can even be elders (bishops) and rule over men. However, in 1 Timothy 3:2 and Titus 1:6, Paul says that an elder must be the husband of one wife. Now how can any woman be the husband of one wife in a relationship that would be acceptable to God? Paul, writing by inspiration, instructed the church at Corinth to, "Let a woman learn quietly with all submissiveness. I do not permit a woman to teach or to exercise authority over a man; rather, she is to remain quiet" (1 Timothy 2:11–12; 1 Cor. 14:34–35; Titus 2:3–5). This male spiritual leadership is not popular with many today. However, it is not man's idea; it is God's idea. It starts with the creation, where Adam came first and then Eve. After they succumbed to the serpent's temptation and sinned, the consequence for Eve was childbearing with pain and subjection to her husband (Gen. 3:16). Many people try to say it is cultural, but it has been this way all the way through history. God instructed Moses to develop an all-male priesthood for the nation of Israel. Jesus chose twelve men to be his apostles and the early church only appointed males as elders. This teaching is not one subject to cultural change. If it were, it would have changed several times by the time we reached the church in the twenty-first century.

God says women should not be elders or preachers, but God does have a plan for women, and that is to teach children and other women, so they grow up understanding who they are and what God wants them to be (Titus 2:3–4). With faithful men and women serving God, a church should be successful in fulfilling its mission for God.

To be a thriving church, the members must have an intense realization of the church's mission. The very reason the church exists is to glorify God in the church. In Ephesians 3:21, Paul says, "to him be glory in the church and Christ Jesus." We lift God up by showing people our zeal and our joy. We tell them about Jesus and that they can have the same joy we have through him. Remember also that God wanted the church here so that it would make known his manifold wisdom (Eph. 3:8–11). The church needs to be committed to do that. Church members need to be dedicated to the worship of the church, its holiness, its compassion, its commitment, its love for God, and its love for brothers and sisters in Christ. He died for us and now we should be alive for him.

A MORAL CHURCH IN AN IMMORAL WORLD

Epistle to Diognetus (c. AD 120–200) is believed to be written by Athenagoras. This section is an important one, as it describes how Christians are alike and different from others.

> For the Christians are distinguished from other men neither by country, nor language, nor the customs which they observe. For they neither inhabit cities of their own, nor employ a peculiar form of speech, nor lead a life which is marked out by any singularity. The course of conduct which they follow has not been devised by any speculation or deliberation of inquisitive men; nor do they, like some, proclaim themselves the advocates of any merely human doctrines. But, inhabiting Greek as well as barbarian cities, according as the lot of each of them has

determined, and following the customs of the natives in respect to clothing, food, and the rest of their ordinary conduct, they display to us their wonderful and confessedly striking method of life. They dwell in their own countries, but simply as sojourners. As citizens, they share in all things with others and yet endure all things as if foreigners. Every foreign land is to them as their native country and every land of their birth as a land of strangers. They marry, as do all [others]; they beget children, but they do not destroy their offspring. They have a common table, but not a common bed. They are in the flesh, but they do not live after the flesh. (2 Cor. 10:3) They pass their days on earth, but they are citizens of heaven. (Phil. 3:20) They obey the prescribed laws, and at the same time surpass the laws by their lives. They love all men and are persecuted by all. They are unknown and condemned; they are put to death and restored to life. (2 Cor. 6:9) They are poor, yet make many rich; (2 Cor. 6:10) they are in lack of all things, and yet abound in all; they are dishonored, and yet in their very dishonor are glorified. They are evil spoken of, and yet are justified; they are reviled, and bless; (2 Cor. 4:12) they are insulted, and repay the insult with honor; they do good, yet are punished as evil-doers. When punished, they rejoice as if quickened into life; they are assailed by the Jews as foreigners, and are persecuted by the Greeks, yet those who hate them are unable to assign any reason for their hatred. (Mathetes 2004)

The world is evil. It is opposed to God and his ways. But the church must be different from the world. Christian lives must be different from the world. Christians must show the world its need for the church in a positive way in order to change the mind of those who make statements like "I love Jesus but hate the church," which is impossible to do. However, while doing this, the church should expect some persecution, especially in our current cultural environment today.

Jesus delivered the church by purchasing it with his blood (Acts 20:28). Paul assures us that Christ gave himself for our sins to deliver us from the present evil age, according to the will of our God and Father (Gal. 1:4). He has delivered us from the domain of darkness and transferred us to the kingdom of his beloved son (Col. 1:13). He bore our sins in his body on the tree that we might die to sin and live to righteousness. By his wounds we are healed (1 Pet. 2:24). Now we must put off the old man, put him to death. (Col. 3:5) Put to death therefore what is earthly in you: sexual immorality, impurity, passion, evil desire, and covetousness, which is idolatry. We bury the dead man (Rom. 6:3), baptize him into his death, and we put on the new man (Rom. 6:4). Paul told the church at Colossae that they had been raised with Christ, and that they should seek the things that are above, where Christ is seated at the right hand of God. They should set their minds on things that are above not on things that are on the earth. For you have died and your life is hidden in Christ (Col. 3:1). We are to walk in obedience (John 14:15; Luke 6:46). As children of light, we stay away from the children of darkness (1 Thess. 5:5–8). They have decided to sleep in sin, but we have chosen salvation.

Time is important. We do not know when God plans to end this world, but when he does, it will be too late to change things. Jesus said, "We must work the works of him who sent us while it is the day; night is coming when no one can work" (John 9:4; Eph. 5:15–16). The church must be vigilant in proclaiming the gospel to the whole world.

The church must know the absolute truth of the gospel; that Jesus is the Christ, the son of God, that he died on a cross so that his blood could wash away our sins, that he was buried and arose three days later, that he was taken up into heaven, and that he sits at the right hand of God acting as our advocate today. The church must know what the will of the Lord is and it must have the courage to live it for itself and to teach it to the world.

Antioch the Evangelistic Church

The city of Antioch lay 300 miles north of Jerusalem. It had a

> population of about half a million people and was known as the Queen of the East and Antioch the Beautiful. It was also noted for its commercialized carnality. It was a great city, rich, and cosmopolitan, and soon to become The Second City of Christianity. (Longenecker 1981, 399)

The church in Antioch began as Christians from the Jerusalem and Cyprus persecutions began to migrate. A large number of disciples and converts soon gathered there. They were ardent disciples, speaking the word, preaching about the Lord, Jesus and being blessed with great success by the hand of the Lord (Acts 11:19–21). They soon distinguished themselves in the Christian brotherhood and received attention and encouragement from Jerusalem in the years following the destruction of Jerusalem in 70 AD. It became the center of Eastern Christianity and had features that need to be reproduced today: a strong evangelistic attitude, a strong self-image, identity with Christ, and being unafraid to show their faith in some risky situations.

They sent out the first organized missionary party to evangelize the world (Acts 13:1–3). They were cosmopolitan, a trait they inherited from Alexander the Great. They were generous, sending aid to those who were starving in Judea. They were God-conscious and knew what they were doing was God's work and not theirs (Acts 13:1–3; 14:26; 15:4, 12). A church preoccupied with meeting its own needs will never be an evangelistic church. A self-conscious group will never leave home. Evangelistic thrust does not come by focusing on ourselves but instead by trusting God and serving others (Matt. 8:19–22). Antioch had a strong self-image and identity. "The disciples were first called Christians at Antioch" (Acts 11:26). That was key to their evangelistic spirit, along with their close identity with Christ. That faith in Christ helped them take strong actions that may have been risky, except for the fact that God was in it with them (Smith 1884).

We need to be like the church at Antioch, but too many are afraid to do any personal evangelism. Those who are afraid need to read Romans 8:12–17,

> So then, brothers, we are debtors, not to the flesh, to live according to the flesh. For if you live according to the flesh you will die, but if by the Spirit you put to death the deeds of the body, you will live. For all who are led by the Spirit of God are sons of God. For you did not receive the spirit of slavery to fall back into fear, but you have received the Spirit of adoption as sons, by whom we cry, 'Abba! Father!' The Spirit himself bears witness with our spirit that we are children of God, and if children, then heirs—heirs of God and fellow heirs with Christ, provided we suffer with him in order that we may also be glorified with him.

We must overcome our fear and teach people how to be saved. Evangelism is personal. It involves people. Christianity is a people thing. It is not a building thing or a business thing or an entertainment thing; it is a people thing. The church is here for people. Jesus came and died for the people. We must concentrate on people. Still, many are afraid to evangelize. They have to trust the Lord and understand that it is the Lord who produces the increase; we just sow the seed (1 Cor. 3:6–7).

Let us examine the Great Commission in Matthew 28:18–20. There are six key points.

1. Jesus has all authority
2. "Go" is an action word that means "while going. We are to teach and baptize as we go along. As we live our lives, we should be seeking opportunities to accomplish this mission to teach the whole world.

3. Make disciples
4. Baptize
5. Teach
6. Heaven Bound

Evangelism must be people-oriented, Christ-centered, and heaven-bound, but many are afraid to do it. Such fear demonstrates a lack of faith in God. God does not hold you responsible for the choice a contact makes, but he does hold you responsible for not trying. Christians should not fear the work that God commands you to do. "For you did not receive the spirit of slavery to fall back into fear, but you have received the Spirit of adoption as sons, by whom we cry, 'Abba! Father!'" (Rom. 8:15). Paul explains to Timothy,

> For God gave us a spirit not of fear but of power and love and self-control. Therefore do not be ashamed of the testimony about our Lord, nor of me his prisoner, but share in suffering for the gospel by the power of God!. (2 Tim. 1:7–8)

The apostle John tells his readers, "There is no fear in love, but perfect love casts out fear. For fear has to do with punishment, and whoever fears has not been perfected in love" (1 John 4:18).

Every Christian should be active in evangelism. If you do not teach, bring your contact to someone who can teach or open your home up for Bible studies or do something that will help lead a contact to Christ. That is the mission Christ gave his church and that is the only way the church can grow.

CHAPTER TEN QUESTIONS

1. Describe the Christian life in the first century as given in the epistle to Diognetus.
2. What equipment has God given us to fight the devil?
3. What do we have to provide in the battle?
4. List nine things needed to have a strong church.
5. Describe the church at Antioch.
6. What keeps many churches from succeeding as Antioch did?
7. Our mission is to _____, God grants the _____
8. What Bible verse should help us overcome the things that keep us from succeeding?
9. List the six points that describe the great commission.

ELEVEN

So How Do We Get A Strong Church?

PUTTING IT BACK TOGETHER

Humpty Dumpty sat on a wall.

Humpty Dumpty had a great fall.

All the king's horses and all the king's men couldn't put Humpty Dumpty together again.

The human condition is broken; it had a great fall. Who can put us back together again? The world's condition is broken; it also had a great fall. Who can put it back together again?

The situation in the world today makes it difficult for churches to work, but that may partly be the church's fault because it has not always been ready for the different cultural changes. It does not matter now; the mission for the church is still there to accomplish and Jesus expects the church to do it.

Humankind needs a healer. Job's friend Bildad describes man's condition when he says, "Behold, even the moon is not bright, and the stars are not pure in his eyes; how much less man, who is a maggot, and the son of man, who is a worm!" (Job 25:5–6). Many have tried the things of today, pop psychology and worldly thoughts. Are we any better? No! We cannot put ourselves back together. The Bible says, "There is a way that seems right to a man, but its end is the way to death" (Prov. 16:25). And God says, "I spread out my hands all the day to a rebellious people, who walk in a way that is not good, following their own devices" (Isa. 65:2). Our devices are killing us. We need a savior, and we have one. He even rides a white horse:

> From his mouth comes a sharp sword with which to strike down the nations and he will rule them with a rod of iron. He will tread the winepress of the fury of the wrath of God the Almighty. On his robe and on his thigh he has a name written, King of kings and Lord of lords. (Rev.19:15–16). He will also defeat all the enemies of righteousness and win a home in heaven for those who honor him.

"They will make war on the Lamb, and the Lamb will conquer them, for he is Lord of lords and King of kings, and those with him are called and chosen and faithful" (Rev. 17:14). Christ will win this spiritual war, and his bride will be right there with him in heaven.

Someone asks the question, "What do we make of Jesus Christ?" C.S. Lewis answered, "This is a question which, in a sense, has a frantically comic side. For the real question is not what are we to make of Christ, but what is He to make of us?" (2014) Actually, what Christ makes of us depends on what we make of him. We need to trust him and follow him because "God has highly exalted him and bestowed on him the name that is above every name, so that at the name of Jesus every knee should bow, in heaven and on earth and under the earth" (Phil. 2:9–10). Matthew tells us about the great power and compassion Jesus has,

> Go and tell John what you hear and see: the blind receive their sight and the lame walk, lepers are cleansed, and the deaf hears, and the dead are raised

up, and the poor have good news preached to them. And blessed is the one who is not offended by me. (Matt.11:4–6)

Jesus, himself pleads with us to let him help us:

> Come to me, all who labor and are heavy laden, and I will give you rest. Take my yoke upon you, and learn from me, for I am gentle and lowly in heart, and you will find rest for your souls. For my yoke is easy, and my burden is light. (Matt. 11:28–30)

We must come to Jesus in our brokenness.

> Asian men, called Berkutchi, capture eagles when they are very young (eagles can live to be 40). The Berkutchi snatch them from their nest or through a baited trap. They put them in a cage on a perch that is constantly swaying, and they put a hood on them for two to three days. They give them no food or water and no rest or sleep, only the swaying. The Berkutchi talk, sing, and chant to the eagle and after a couple of days, when the eagle gets weak, he is finally fed a little and petted. The bird then begins to rely on his master. When the relationship is right, the training begins. Not all eagles will train, but those who take to life with their master display intense loyalty (Cynthia 2018).

This training may seem harsh, but when we are broken is when we will realize our dependence on God and will become close to him. David's experience in Psalm 51 is an example: "Create in me a clean heart, O God, and renew a right spirit within me. Cast me not away from your presence, and take not your Holy Spirit from me. Restore to me the joy of your salvation, and uphold me with a willing spirit"

(Ps. 51:10–12). God also reminded the apostle Paul about his need for God when he told him, "My grace is sufficient for you for my power is made perfect in weakness" (2 Cor. 12:9). Therefore, God fixes the broken man with Jesus; how does he fix a broken world? The same way as he fixes humankind.

> One Sunday morning, a man woke up when his wife and children are still asleep. Glad to have time to himself, he went downstairs, brewed some coffee, and began to read the morning paper. Three sentences into an article, he saw his five-year-old daughter descending the stairs. He said, "Honey, go back to bed." "But I'm not sleepy," she insisted. Determined to read his paper, he again urged her to go back to bed. Again, she told him she was not tired. Looking down at the newspaper, he conceived a plan. In the paper was a picture of the world, which he cut into several pieces. Handing his daughter some tape, he instructed her, "Go sit in the dining room and see if you can put the world back together."
>
> His daughter accepted the challenge, and he went back to the kitchen to finish his coffee and read the paper. After only a few sips of his coffee, his daughter came bounding into the kitchen. "Here, Daddy, I'm finished!" she said, showing him the picture of the world put back together. Amazed, he asked, "Sweetie, how did you do that so fast?" She replied, "It was easy, Daddy. On the backside of the page was a picture of a man. When you make the man right, you make the world right" (Ellis 2001).

In a similar way, only Jesus can bring order to this world. God uses broken things—broken soil to produce a crop, broken clouds to give rain, broken grain to give bread, broken bread to give strength, broken alabaster box to give perfume. It is Peter, weeping bitterly, who returns to greater power than ever (Havner 2019).

Jesus became what we are so he might make us what he is. Jesus prays to his Father, "As you sent me into the world, so I have sent them into the world" (John 17:18). The apostle Paul was sent into the world by Jesus. He was happy to go, "I have been crucified with Christ. It is no longer I who live, but Christ who lives in me. And the life I now live in the flesh I live by faith in the Son of God, who loved me and gave himself for me" (Gal. 2:20). Jesus gave his all for humankind and for this world. Many people did not believe in him when he came, and many still do not believe in him. Nevertheless, the world would be a much better place to live if people followed him and became one of his citizens. He went from being the king of all things to a man, to a servant, to a cross, and back to a being a king.

Imagine a world of people like Jesus, who have the fruit of the spirit (Gal. 5:22–23), which is love, joy, peace, patience, kindness, goodness, faithfulness, gentleness, and self-control. It would be great! Yes, it would indeed be heaven on earth.

CHAPTER ELEVEN QUESTIONS

1. How does Bildad describe man's condition?
2. Can man fix his problems by himself? (Prov. 16:25; Isa. 65:2)
3. What verse tells us about Jesus helping us in times of need?
4. How does the Berkutchi story relate to Christ's help for us?
5. How can the church fix the world today? (Gal. 2:20)
6. Jesus became what we are so he might _____ us what he is.
7. Just think what the world would be like if _____.

TWELVE

The Church Must Accomplish Its Mission

The Bible was written to be obeyed, and not simply studied. That is why the words, 'therefore,' and 'wherefore,' are repeated so often in the second half of Ephesians (4:1, 17. 25, 5:1, 7, 14, 17, 24). Paul is saying, 'here is what Christ has done for you. Now, in the light of this, here is what we ought to do for Christ.' (Wiersbe 1985, 107)

What should the church do to please Christ? They can be kind, tenderhearted, and forgiving to one another, as God in Christ forgave them. "Let all bitterness and wrath and anger and clamor and slander be put away from you, along with all malice. Be kind to one another, tenderhearted, forgiving one another, as God in Christ forgave you" (Eph. 4:31–32). Note the words "kind" and "tenderhearted" (compassion). Also, Paul reminds us that, "while we were still weak, at the right time, Christ died for the ungodly" (Rom. 5:6). Kindness, compassion, and forgiveness are all traits one must use in the church if the church is to fulfill its mission and glorify God.

Paul reminded the Roman church that they should welcome one another as Christ has welcomed you, for the glory of God. We must accept one another; there can be no prejudices in the Lord's church. "In him, you also are being built together into a dwelling place for God by the Spirit." He also said in Galatians 3:26–28,

> For in Christ Jesus you are all sons of God, through faith. For as many of you as were baptized into Christ have put on Christ. There is neither Jew nor Greek; there is neither slave nor free, there is no male and female, for you are all one in Christ Jesus.

We must remember that the saved are in Christ, and Galatians 3:27 says that when we are baptized, we put on Christ. There is no putting on Christ without baptism.

We must understand our freedom in Christ. "For you were called to freedom, brethren. Only do not use your freedom as an opportunity for the flesh, but through love serve one another." We must serve one another in love and liberty." (Rom. 8:13–14; 1 Cor. 13: 1–8).

From Philippians 2:3, we learn, "do nothing from selfish ambition or conceit but in humility count others more significant than yourselves." The humble person is not one who thinks meanly of himself; he simply does not think of himself at all. Humility is that grace that when you know you have it, you lose it.

The truly humble person knows himself and accepts who he is. "For by the grace given to me, I say to everyone among you not to think of himself more highly than he ought to think, but to think with sober judgment, each according to the measure of faith that God has assigned" (Rom. 12:3). Paul speaks of losing everything again: "because of the passing worth of knowing Christ Jesus our Lord. For his sake, I have suffered the loss of all things and count them as rubbish, in order that I may gain Christ" (Phil. 3:8). The church needs people who are willing to make the sacrifice to serve God like the apostle Paul did. Often times, when I speak, I emphasize the fact that things do not matter. We humans want to make everything something, but nothing that happens to us in this world matters in the end. If you are a genuine Christian, you will go to heaven, and that should bring joy to your heart. If you are not Christian or if you are a lukewarm Christian

(Rev. 3:15–17), you will be destined for eternal punishment and there will be no joy.

Paul tells us of another attitude and maybe the most difficult one Christians must have if the church is to succeed in fulfilling Christ's mission. That attitude is forgiveness. He says, "bearing with one another and, if one has a complaint against another, forgiving each other; as the Lord has forgiven you, so you also must forgive" (Col. 3:13). He also mentions longsuffering to the Roman church, "or do you presume on the riches of his kindness and forbearance and patience, not knowing that God's kindness is meant to lead you to repentance" (Rom. 2:4). Members of the church need to be patient with God and with each other. They must not quit on people, the church, or the Lord. We need to remember that we go through trials in this world to prove and strengthen our faith. We need to memorize this verse and keep it close to help us overcome temptation: "No temptation has overtaken you that is not common to man. God is faithful, and he will not let you be tempted beyond your ability, but with the temptation, he will also provide the way of escape, that you may be able to endure it" (1 Cor. 10:13). Do you see that God is always helping us? We just have to do our part by following his orders, and he will be there to help us. Now, whether we accept his help or not is another question.

I have been trying to get this older man to go to church with me for years, but just a couple of days ago, when I asked him again about going to church, he said, "God has not told me too." To which, I said, "No, he told me to tell you." He chuckled and said maybe, but he still has not bothered to come to church. I guess he believes God will personally tell him to go to church, but I do know that God tells me to encourage him to go to church. He just does not know God's word or his ways. He is just like the people back in Nehemiah's day who did not know the law. Here, the difference is that when they heard the law, they obeyed. When we hear the law of Christ, we simply ignore it.

Nevertheless, forgiveness is an attitude of the heart for those who profess to be members of the Lord's church and have the mind of Christ.

For a church to be successful in carrying out the mission of Christ, it must maintain a clean slate. The members must be willing to confess, and there are two types of confession.

First, they must be willing to confess their belief in Jesus Christ as the son of God. In the first century, it was dangerous for one to admit that he was a Christian because it could cost them dearly. Their family could cast them out; if they owned a business, the community could boycott them; and the community could have them thrown in prison or put to death. To make that confession was a very serious thing and only committed Christians would do it. They must also be willing to confess their sins and repent of them. Confessions of sin keep the slate clean, and the disciple can continue to do the work of the Lord without guilt weighing him down.

THE MISSION

The mission as Jesus gave it to us is to proclaim the gospel message to the whole world. The church does it by proclamation both in the worship service and by individual efforts. Christians call it evangelizing. It means to bear the good news to someone (vines n.d., 384). There are three certainties in evangelism in the New Testament that need to be understood by the church. They are as follows:

1. All accountable, responsible souls are lost without the gospel.
2. The power of God unto salvation is in the gospel (Rom. 1:16).
3. God has a plan, a method. He chose his apostles to carry on with this plan after he returned to heaven (Matt. 28:18–20), but he also set up a kingdom, the church, with the same charge that he gave his apostles—to take the gospel to the whole world.

> How beautiful upon the mountains are the feet of him who brings good news, who publishes peace, who brings good news of happiness, who publishes salvation, who says to Zion, "Your God reigns." (Isa. 52:7)

> For "everyone who calls on the name of the Lord will be saved." How then will they call on him in whom they have not believed, and how are they to believe in him of whom they have never heard? And, how are they to hear without someone preaching? And how are they to preach unless they are sent? As it is written, "How beautiful are the feet of those who preach the good news!" (Rom. 10:13–15)

Jesus issued this mission to his apostles four times: "Thus it is written, that the Christ should suffer and on the third day rise from the dead, and that repentance and forgiveness of sins should be proclaimed in his name to all nations, beginning from Jerusalem. You are witnesses to these things" (Luke 24:46–48). He said to them:

> Go into all the world and proclaim the gospel to the whole creation. Whoever believes and is baptized will be saved, but whoever does not believe will be condemned. (Mark 16:15–16)

> Go therefore and make disciples of all nations, baptizing them in the name of the Father and of the Son and of the Holy Spirit, teaching them to observe all that I have commanded you. And behold, I am with you always, to the end of the age. (Matt. 28:19–20)

Jesus said to them again, "Peace be with you. As the Father has sent me, even so, I am sending you" (John 20:21). Paul told Timothy, "and what you have heard from me in the presence of many witnesses entrust to faithful men who will be able to teach others also" (2 Timothy 2:2).

What a great result came from this plan. In the book of Acts we find:

- 2:41: 3000 souls were saved
- 4:4: 5000 souls were saved
- 5:14: "more than ever believers were added to the Lord"
- 6:7: "the Word continued to increase, and the number of the disciples multiplied greatly in Jerusalem, and a great many of the priests became obedient to the faith."
- 8:1–4: "Now those who were scattered went about preaching the word" So the church throughout all Judea and Galilee and Samaria had peace and was being built up. And walking in the fear of the Lord and in the comfort of the Holy Spirit, it multiplied" (Acts 9:31).

God's plan worked superbly and by 2000, there were roughly 2,000,000,000 Christians in the world. This plan must go on, but we have too many Christians who do not take every opportunity to teach the gospel to the lost. This has to stop. We have to make contacts with people and try to lead them to Christ.

BEING A PILLAR IN GOD'S HOUSE

God wants to make known his saving presence in the world. In the Old Testament, he did it through the temple, but today he does it through his church.

> So then, you are no longer strangers and aliens, but you are fellow citizens with the saints and members of the household of God, built on the foundation of the apostles and prophets, Christ Jesus himself being the cornerstone, in whom the whole structure, being joined together, grows into a holy temple in the Lord. In him, you also are being built together into a dwelling place for God by the Spirit. (Eph. 2:19–22)

Even though this is God's purpose and it is what the world needs, many churches are desolate. They have a few conversions, inadequate funds, low attendance, half-hearted worship, and few outsiders visit.

There was a small period of time in Israel's history when the temple was desolate. God sent a prophet to explain to the people why. We can learn from this prophet why today's church can be desolate.

In Haggai 1:1–11, God says to Haggai and his people that the reason his temple was not finished was that they were building their own houses and not taking the temple seriously. They cared more about their own stuff than they did God's.

God's ultimate priority for his people is that they would advance his kingdom in the world. "But, seek first the kingdom of God and His righteousness, and all these things will be added to you" (Matt. 6:33). The church can only be built by disciples making disciples.

> Go therefore and make disciples of all nations, baptizing them in the name of the Father and of the Son and of the Holy Spirit, teaching them to observe all that I have commanded you. And behold, I am with you always, to the end of the age. (Matt. 28:19-20)

The church can only be built by disciples managing their spiritual gifts (Eph. 4:11–13).

> And he gave the apostles, the prophets, the evangelists, the shepherds and teachers, to equip the saints for the work of ministry, for building up the body of Christ, until we all attain to the unity of the faith and of the knowledge of the Son of God, to mature manhood, to the measure of the stature of the fullness of Christ.

In his parable of the talents, the Lord teaches that one should use his talents to grow the kingdom of God on the earth. Both the five-talent servant and the two-talent servant doubled their talents and were rewarded with a home by their Lord. The one-talent man did not trust his master and was afraid he would lose his talent and be punished. The master was very upset with him for not using his one talent to increase what he had, so he was "cast into outer darkness where there would be weeping and gnashing of teeth." I wonder where that place may be; I do not want to go there. James also warns us, "So whoever knows the right thing to do and fails to do it, for him it is a sin" (James 4:17).

Paul tells us also, "Moreover, it is required of stewards that they are found faithful" (1 Cor. 4:2). James and Paul tell us how things should be, but we look around, and too many Christians are like the exiles who came back from Babylon in Haggai's day. They are too busy taking care of themselves and leaving God's work undone. God does see through our excuses. Deep down, the reason we are not working for God is a problem of the heart. Our priorities are wrong.

> Behold, a lawyer stood up to put him to the test, saying, "Teacher, what shall I do to inherit eternal life?" He said to him, "What is written in the Law? How do you read it?" He answered, "You shall love the Lord your God with all your heart and with all your soul and with all your strength and with all your mind, and your neighbor as yourself." "And he said to him, 'You have answered correctly; do this, and you will live." (Luke 10:25–28)

THREE LOVES OF A DISCIPLE

1. A disciple loves the Lord. Everyone who believes that Jesus is the Christ has been born of God, and everyone who loves the Father loves whoever has been born of him. By this, we know that we love the children of God when we love God and obey his commandments. For this is the love of God, that we keep his commandments. And his commandments are not burdensome (1 John 5:1–3).

2. A disciple loves the brethren. Beloved, if God so loved us, we also ought to love one another (1 John 4:11).
3. A disciple loves the lost. "Brothers, my heart's desire and prayer to God for them is that they may be saved" (Rom. 10:1) (Copeland 2016).

To those who say they love Jesus and hate the church–Why not obey the gospel and be added to the church and help fight for Jesus' way in his army? Help the church make known the manifold wisdom of God and bring the kingdom of heaven to this world as Jesus prayed would happen.

To those who say they have found another way to express their faith without going to church, I say this: You can express your faith somewhere else all you want to, but if you continue to stay away and hurt the blood-bought church of Christ, God will one day bring his wrath down upon you, and say to you, "now you know that I am the Lord."

CHAPTER TWELVE QUESTIONS

1. What should the church do to please Christ?
2. What does Paul say about forgiving? (Rom. 15:7)
3. The church needs people who will _____ and _____ the church like the apostle Paul did.
4. List the three certainties in evangelism that must be understood by the church.
5. List the four verses where Jesus issued this evangelistic message to the apostles.
6. How successful was this plan?
7. God wants to make known his _____ presence in the world.
8. Why can the church not get this done today? (Hag. 1:1–11)
9. How much are we to love the Lord?

THIRTEEN

The Church, The Gate To Heaven

GENESIS 28:17

Genesis chapter 28 is the story of Jacob's ladder. Jacob, as he was on the way to pick a wife, goes to sleep and dreams that there is a ladder coming down from heaven and the angels are going up and down the ladder, in and out of heaven. He sees God standing at the top. God speaks to Jacob and tells him that he will bless him, and give him all the land of Canaan just as he had promised his grandfather, Abraham, and his father, Isaac. Jacob was so taken by this that he said, "Surely the Lord is in this place, and I did not know it. Moreover, he was afraid and said, 'How awesome is this place! This is none other than the house of God, and this is the gate of heaven.'" John Gill describes the meaning of this dream,

> Because the heavens were opened and the glory of God was seen attended by his angels, who were coming and going, as people through the streets of a city; and was an emblem of the church of Christ, who is figured by the ladder set on earth, whose top reached to heaven, the door, the gate, the way of ascent to heaven is through the church. (2002)

Remember that Jesus said he would build his church and would give the keys of the kingdom (church) to his disciples (Matt. 16:18–19). This was prophesied by Isaiah (Isa. 22:22) when God said, "I will place on his shoulder the key of the house of David. He shall open, and none shall shut, and he shall shut, and none shall open." The apostle John also speaks of this in Revelation 3:7 "And to the angel of the church in Philadelphia write: 'The words of the holy one, the true one, who has the key of David, who opens and no one will shut, who shuts and no one opens."

This was God's plan all along. Jesus even assures his disciples in (Luke 12:32), "Fear not, little flock, for it is your Father's good pleasure to give you the kingdom." The disciples would then teach others who would teach others and so on, until the apostles all died and the church would continue with the teaching of the gospel. Remember also that Paul described the mission of the church as to make known the manifold wisdom of God (Eph. 3:10). Therefore, the church now has the key and the responsibility to continue the mission of spreading God's wisdom and the gospel of Christ all over the world. Jesus says he came to seek and save the lost (Luke 19:10); the church must seek and save the lost. God loves all people even though they are sinners; the church must love all people, even sinners. Jesus said,

> Come to me, all who labor and are heavy laden, and I will give you rest. Take my yoke upon you, and learn from me, for I am gentle and lowly in heart, and you will find rest for your souls. For my yoke is easy, and my burden is light. (Matt. 11:28–30)

That is the message the church must deliver to the world. The church must hold up the doctrine of Christ. We must do everything under the authority of Christ. He is the way, truth, and life (John 14:6). All authority was given to him (Matt. 28:18), and he tells the church to go into all nations teaching and baptizing.

Christ left the church to teach the way he wanted to save people. He says we must believe in him; "you will die in your sins; unless you believe in me you will die in your sins" (John 8:24). He says we must repent (turn from sin to his righteousness); "The times of ignorance God overlooked, but now he commands all people everywhere to repent" (Acts 17:30). He wants us to confess our belief before other people; "So everyone who acknowledges me before men, I also will acknowledge before my Father who is in heaven, but whoever denies me before men, I also will deny before my Father who is in heaven" (Matt. 10:32–33). He says we must be baptized to wash away our sins (Acts 22:16). Also Peter reminds us about the people of Noah's day, "which sometimes were disobedient, when once the longsuffering of God waited in the days of Noah, while the ark was a preparing, wherein few, that is, eight souls were saved by water" (1 Pet. 3:20–21, KJV).

Baptism, which corresponds to this, now saves you, not like removal of dirt from the body but as an appeal to God for a good conscience, through the resurrection of Jesus Christ (1 Pet. 3:21).

Once one obeys the gospel, he should live according to the guidelines that Christ gives.

> Or do you not know that the unrighteous will not inherit the kingdom of God? Do not be deceived: neither the sexually immoral, nor idolaters, nor adulterers, nor men who practice homosexuality, nor thieves, nor the greedy, nor drunkards, nor revilers, nor swindlers will inherit the kingdom of God. And such were some of you. But you were washed, you were sanctified, you were justified in the name of the Lord Jesus Christ and by the Spirit of our God. (1 Cor.6:9–11)

Christians do not live unrighteous lives; they should want to live the righteous life for Christ and their salvation.

When one obeys the gospel, Christ grants his presence with them. He adds them to his church. He indulges them with communion with him (Luke. 22:15–16). He lets us know that he stands at the door and knocks and if we open the door, he will come in and eat with us in that communion (Rev. 3:20). Christ wants to be with his people. Remember, he bought the church with his own blood (Acts 20:28). He also promises to be with us when two or three are gathered together (Matt. 18:20). Therefore, you know he will be with you in his church.

The church is the body of Christ, the bride of Christ, and the kingdom of Christ. Christ loves the church, nourishes the church, and cherishes the church. The church is an important part of his plan of salvation. It takes his message to the whole world. If you say you do not need the church or say you hate the church or just are not interested in the church, then you might as well claim not to be a Christian because Christ is in the church all day, every day. Please go to church and help make the world a better place.

You may see people who are supposedly Christians and attend church do bad things, or get in an argument or indulge in some other wrongdoing and think that the church is not good. Please remember that Christians are still people living in the flesh and as long as we are in the flesh, we will make mistakes. But then again, that is why we are in the church. We can get forgiveness there and help overcome trials and tribulations.

> But if we walk in the light, as he is in the light, we have fellowship with one another, and the blood of Jesus his Son cleanses us from all sin. If we say we have no sin, we deceive ourselves, and the truth is not in us. If we confess our sins, he is faithful and just to forgive us our sins and to cleanse us from all unrighteousness. If we say we have not sinned, we make him a liar, and his word is not in us. (1 John 1:7–10)

John said this to Christians in the church at Ephesus.

Who Will Enter the Kingdom of Heaven?

The following verses give us an idea of who will enter the kingdom of heaven.

> For I tell you unless your righteousness exceeds that of the scribes and Pharisees, you will never enter the kingdom of heaven. (Matt. 5:20)

> Not everyone who says to me, "Lord, Lord," will enter the kingdom of heaven, but the one who does the will of my Father who is in heaven. (Matt.7:21)

> Truly, I say to you, unless you turn and become like children, you will never enter the kingdom of heaven. (Matt.18:3)

> And Jesus said to his disciples, "Truly, I say to you, only with difficulty will a rich person enter the kingdom of heaven." (Matt.19:23)

> But woe to you, scribes and Pharisees, hypocrites! For you shut the kingdom of heaven in people's faces. For you neither enter yourselves nor allow those who would enter to go in. (Matt.23:13)

The last verse is what the denominational churches do by telling people that they can be saved without obeying God's command to be baptized and also that once they are saved, they cannot fall.

In James 2:17 we find that faith without works is dead. Yet, so many teach that one can be saved by faith only without any action on our part. This doctrine is the same spirit that was being spread in Jeremiah's day when God chastised the Jews for their idol worship:

> The word that came to Jeremiah from the Lord: 'Stand in the gate of the Lord's house, and proclaim

there this word, and say, hear the word of the Lord, all you men of Judah who enter these gates to worship the Lord. Thus says the Lord of hosts, the God of Israel: Amend your ways and your deeds, and I will let you dwell in this place. Do not trust in these deceptive words: 'This is the temple of the Lord, the temple of the Lord, the temple of the Lord. (Jer. 7:1–4)

There was only one temple of the Lord; all the others were idol-worshipping temples. The same is true today; there is only one church, not thousands of them. John the Baptist even said to the Jews, "Say not to yourselves we be Abraham's sons."

There are many false teachers in the world trying to draw us away from the truth, but we have to study for ourselves and decide what the absolute truth is. We must examine the scriptures to see whether or not they are telling the truth. We need to study the doctrines of a church we think about attending to make sure it is scriptural. We should not choose a church because they have a really nice building or good music. We also should not choose a church because they helped us out of some kind of life situation. We even should not choose a church because our parents or our spouse go there. One cannot go to heaven based on their parent's faith; it must be on their own faith. We need to choose a church that has the right doctrine. The things they teach and do need to match what the Bible says.

The kingdom of God is present now but chiefly future. "But according to his promise we are waiting for new heavens and a new earth in which righteousness dwells. Therefore, beloved, since you are waiting for these, be diligent to be found by him without spot or blemish, and at peace" (2 Pet. 3:13–14).

> Blessed be the God and Father of our Lord Jesus Christ! According to his great mercy, he has caused us to be born again to a living hope through the resurrection of Jesus Christ from the dead, to an inheritance that is imperishable, undefiled, and unfading, kept in heaven

for you, who by God's power are being guarded through faith for a salvation ready to be revealed in the last time. (1 Pet. 1:3–5)

The Bible speaks of heaven, the heavenly life, and joys. It is a place where there is no night, no sin, no cursing, and no pain. John describes it as a place where God "will wipe away every tear from their eyes, and death shall be no more, neither shall there be mourning, nor crying, nor pain anymore, for the former things, have passed away" (Rev. 21:4). Jesus says "there are many mansions there" (John 14:1–2). It is the eternal home where we shall see Him face to face. The unrighteous will not inherit it.

> Or do you not know that the unrighteous will not inherit the kingdom of God? Do not be deceived: neither the sexually immoral, nor idolaters, nor adulterers, nor men who practice homosexuality, nor thieves, nor the greedy, nor drunkards, nor revilers, nor swindlers will inherit the kingdom of God. And such were some of you. But you were washed, you were sanctified, you were justified in the name of the Lord Jesus Christ and by the Spirit of our God. (1 Cor. 6:9–11)

Corinth had been noted for things mentioned above (vv. 9–10), and many of their Christians were guilty of them before they obeyed the gospel. However, that big three letter word, "but," emphasizes the contrast between their present state and past and the consequent demand that their changed condition made on them.

They were washed, just like the apostle Paul in Acts 22:16. He was told to "arise and be baptized and wash away your sins." Timothy was also instructed on the need for this cleansing, "Therefore, if anyone cleanses himself from what is dishonorable, he will be a vessel for honorable use, set apart as holy, useful to the master of the house, ready for every good work" (2 Tim.2:21). Their seeking for the forgiveness offered by the gospel was fulfilled by divinely ordained conditions, and they actually received forgiveness of their sins (Mark 16:15–16; Acts 2:38). By being cleansed in baptism, they were also sanctified, set apart for a life of holiness. "…who gave himself for us to redeem us from all lawlessness and to purify for himself a people for his own possession who are zealous for good works" (Titus 2:14). They were also justified in the name of the Lord Jesus Christ. As servants of Jesus Christ, they were justified as having passed from a condition of guilty sinners to that of pardoned children of God. Those who do what these Corinthians did will enter the kingdom of God.

The New Testament does not envision solitary religion; some kind of regular assembly for worship and instruction everywhere was taken for granted in the Epistles. Therefore, we must be regular practicing members of the church. Of course, we differ in temperament. Some (like you and me) find it more natural to approach God in solitude, but we must go to church as well.

> For the church is not a human society of people united by their natural affinities but the Body of Christ, in which all members, however different, (and He rejoices in their differences and by no means wishes to iron them out) must share the common life, complementing and helping one another precisely by their differences. (Lewis 2014)

WE CANNOT GO TO HEAVEN WITHOUT GOING TO CHURCH!

CHAPTER THIRTEEN QUESTIONS

1. Describe your thoughts about Jacob's dream.
2. Who did Christ give the keys to the kingdom?
3. When was this planned?
4. Who is to "make known the manifold wisdom of God today"? (Eph. 3:10)
5. Write down the plan of salvation Jesus taught for the church to make known to the world.
6. Since there are many false teachers out there, how do we know which church to choose?
7. We must do everything under the _____ of Jesus.
8. List the verses that tell us who will enter the kingdom of heaven.
9. Will the unrighteous enter heaven?
10. Let's pass righteous judgment on the Corinthians (1 Cor. 6:9–11). Will they make it to heaven? Yes/No

BIBLIOGRAPHY

Barna, George. *Think Like Jesus.* Brentwood: Integrity, 2003.

Bitter, Gregg. *Sermon Central.com.* 2010. Accessed December 24, 2018. https://www.sermancentral.com/.

Bruce, F.F. 1977. *Paul: Apostle of the Heart Set Free.* Grand Rapids: Eerdmans, 2018.

Brueggeman, Walter. "The Congregation and the Crisis of Modernity." Page 139 in *Preaching as a Social Act: Theology and Practice.* Edited by Arthur Van Seters. N.p.:Abingdon, 1988.

Copeland, Mark A. "The Three Loves of a Disciple." 2016. Accessed January 10, 2019. http://executableoutlines.com/top/3loves.htm.

Croeschel, Craig. "God Is Not Calling Us to Go to Church." http://WWW.Bing.Com/discover/god-calls?First=1&tab=REC.

Cynthia and Niko. "Journal of Nomads." 2018. Accessed January 10, 2019. https://www.journalofnomads.com/eagle-hunters-kyrgyzstan/.

Davis, John D. "Holy." *Davis Dictionary of the Bible.* Grand Rapids: Baker, 1980.

Dryden. *"Inspire."* Www.webster-dictionary.net, 2014.

Ellis, Steve. "Preaching Today." 2001. Accessed January 10, 2019. https://www.preachingtoday.com/illustrations/2001/september/13269.html.

Frances, John Di. *Reclaiming the Ethical High Ground.* Delafield: Reliance, 2002.

Gibson, Troy. "The Reformed Mind." 2011. Accessed December 25, 2018. https://thereformedmind.wordpress.com/.

Gill, John. *Zondervan Illustrated Bible Backgrounds Commentary of the Old Testament – House of God … gate of heaven (Gen 28:17).* 2002. Accessed January 19, 2019. https://www.biblegateway.com/resources/zibbc-ot/house-of-god-gate-of-heaven-gen-28-17.

Gray, Alice. "Seeing God." Pages 18-19 in *More Stories for the Heart.* Colorado Springs: Multnomah, 1993.

Havner, Vance. "preachingtoday.com." 2019. Accessed January 10, 2019. https://www.preachingtoday.com/search/?type= author&query=Vance Havner, Leadership, Vol. 4, no. 1.& order=rating&sourcename=all.

Helbock, Thomas A. "Insight on Tolerance." *Cross and Crescent*, Summer: 2. 1996.

Herrick, Greg. "Bible.Org." 2004. Accessed December 22, 2018. https://biblc.org/seriespage/8-ecclesiology-church.

Hodge, Charles. *My Daily Walk with God.* Searcy: Resource, 2000.

Holy Bible American Standard Version. Fort Worth: Star, 1901.

Holy Bible, King James Version. Nashville: Broadman and Holman, 1996.

Holy Bible English Standard Version. Wheaton, IL: Crossway, 2001.

Hunt, T. W. *The Mind of Christ.* Nashville: Broadman and Holman, 1995.

Longenecker, Richard N. "Acts of the Apostles." Pages 205-273 in vol. 9, part 2 of *The Expositor's Bible Commentary.* Edited by Frank Gaebelein. Grand Rapids: Zondervan, 1981.

Lynn, Mac. "Church Growth, The Right Direction." *Missions Bulletin* 4, November 1978.

Mathetes. "Epistle to Diognetus" In *e-sword Reference Library, Ante-Nicene Fathers, V. 1, 1.02-02*. Edited by Philip Shaffer. Vers. 2004. Accessed January 24, 2019. www.e-sword.net.

May, Cecil. *Bible Questions and Answers*. Montgomery: Faulkner University, 2012.

McCallum, Dennis. *The Death of Truth*. Minneapolis: Bethany House, 1996.

McDowell, Josh, and Bob Hostetler. *The New Tolerance*. Wheaton: Tyndale, 1998.

Minear, Paul S. *Images of the Church in the New Testament*. Philadelphia: Westminster, 1960.

Moulton, Harold K., ed. *The Analytical Greek Lexicon Revised*. Grand Rapids: Zondervan, 1979.

Packer, J. I. *Knowing God*. Downers Grove: Intervarsity, 1973.

Pannenberg, Wolfhart. *101 Quotes That Connect*. Grand Rapids: Zondervan, 2009.

Ravenhill, Leonard. *Why Revival Tarries*. Minneapolis: Bethany House, 1959.

"Regional Distribution, Religion in Public Life." Pew Research Center, Washington, D.C., 2011. Accessed January 24, 2019. www.pewforum.org.

Shatner, William. *https://www.preachingtoday.com/search/?type= &pinterest-extension-installed=ms1.39.1&query= Star%20Trek%20V.* 1989. Accessed January 10, 2019. https://www.preachingtoday.com/search/?query=Star%20Trek%20V&type=.

Smith, F. LaGard. *The Cultural Church*. Nashville: 20th Century Christian, 1992.

Smith, James Bryan. *The Good and Beautiful Community.* Downers Grove: IVP, 2010.

Stott, John. *The Radical Disciple.* Downers Grove: IVP, 2001.

Thayer, Joseph Henry. Greek - English Lexicon of the New Testament. Grand Rapids: Zondervan, 1982. Pages 575–576.

Thayer, Smith. *The New NAS Greek Lexicon entry for Protos.* 1999. Accessed December 17, 2018.

Thompson, James W. *Preaching Like Paul.* Louisville: Westminster John Knox, 2001.

Tinkler, Marc. "Vocabulary.com." 1996. Accessed January 16, 2019. www.vocabulary.com/dictionary/lackadaisical.

"Tolerate." *Webster New World Dictionary of English Words 3rd ed.*

Trish, Cyprian. "Lovedazelot." 2009. Accessed December 20, 2019. Lovedazelot.blogspot.com/2009/07/letter-from-st-cyprian-to-donatus-1st.htm.

Vinc, W. E. "*proskuneo,* worship." Vine's expository Dictionary of New Testament Words. McLean: MacDonald, n.d.

"Why Americans Go (and Don't Go) to Religious Services." Pew Research Center, Washington, D.C., 2018. Accessed January 10, 2019. http://www.pewforum.org/2018/08/01/why-americans-go-to-religious-services/.

Wiersbe, Warren W. *Be Rich.* Wheaton: Victor Books, 1985.

Willard, Dallas. *The Spirit of the Disciplines.* San Francisco: Harper, 1988.